<u>2007.</u>

To Suzy,

I've read you enough
of these. I figured you
deserved your own
copy.

Of course, we both
already know that
the world is mad.
This is just further
evidence.

Merry Christmas,

Love, Jim

1

It Must Be True...
I Read It In
The Tabloids

Edited by Mark Williams

First published in Great Britain in November 2006
by Dennis Publishing
30 Cleveland Street, London W1T 4JD

© 2006 Dennis Publishing Ltd

The moral right of the authors has been asserted

Special thanks to Seth Hawthorne and Etienne Gilfillan

A CIP catalogue record for this book is available from
the British Library.

ISBN 0 9516709 5 6

Designed by Andrew Riley
Cartoons by Simon Pearsall
Jacket Design by Richard Adams Associates
Cover Illustration by Andy Martin

Printed and Bound in Great Britain by Mackays of Chatham

Trade Distribution in the UK by Pan Macmillan

INTRODUCTION

In The Week's first few issues, our column of news from the tabloids had aliens dropping in on Britain to ravish its women, a young "Romeo" proposing marriage by bending over to reveal a tattoo on his bottom that read "Connie will you marry me?", a bored wife advertising for a "potent partner" and finding that the naked man who turned up in a hotel room in response to the ad was her husband, and a new craze in California for "moonbathing" as a way of getting a tan at night without the risk of getting skin cancer.

That was summer 1995. Have things changed? Not much. The same assortment of failed crooks, eccentric lovers and weirdoes of all kinds is still making headlines. Looking a recent issue of The Week as I write this, I find a Chinese man has put up his soul for sale on the internet, an academic in India has suggested that donkeys make better companions than wives ("While the housewife may complain and walk off to her parents' home, you will never catch the donkey being disloyal"), and an American policeman who shot himself in the foot is suing his employers for causing him "mental anguish".

How to deal with the tabloids was one of the trickier questions I faced when I dreamt up The Week. With their forthright columnists and no-nonsense editorials, they were obviously going to be important in our coverage of major stories, but in many ways the world they represent is very different from the world of the broadsheets. I thought the best way to capture this was in a separate column; whatever else, the tabloids make our lives a little more entertaining – which, I hope, is what this book, drawn from the first ten years of The Week, will do for you.

Jolyon Connell - Founder

EDITOR'S NOTE

Compiling this book necessarily involved delving into over five hundred back issues of The Week, a time-consuming process rendered far from arduous owing to the gloriously bizarre nature of the material to hand. Indeed my real difficulty lay in limiting the number that I could include in this not-so slim volume, but knowing when to stop was ultimately governed by a vicious production schedule. Which is why February 2006 was when I bolted the door on further entries and settled down to try and muster the widest variety of (allegedly) true stories that only the tabloids could trawl up, and of course the funniest ones. But if any of your favourites failed to make it, by this time next year there'll be many hundreds more to choose from, and so with all the brazenness of a tabloid editor, I'd therefore recommend that you subscribe to The Week immediately !

Mark Williams – May 2006

CONTENTS

Pearsall.

Pet Power

Anne Orsinga, 60, chairman of a bird protection society in Holland, has been taken to hospital with concussion and a broken cheekbone after a dead goose fell 75ft from the sky and hit her on the head.
Issue 31: Dec 23rd 1995

Alfred Larnette, from New York, is being charged with animal cruelty after he entered a lion's cage and bit off one of its ears. The lion was a neighbour's pet and had annoyed Larnette by roaring all night.
Issue 32: Jan 6th 1996

Rara, a penguin, has been trained to waddle down to the local fishmonger to get his own dinner. Owner Yukio Mishimoto of Shibushi, Japan, said: "Rara has a little backpack, and comes home with sardines and a mackerel."
Issue 75: Nov 2nd 1996

Horse-mad Kim Hunter, 30, has chosen her pony Floral Dance to be her bridesmaid when she marries John Coppen at Marks Tey, Essex.
Issue 108: June 28th 1997

After neighbours complained of the smell from widow Vivian Parson's house in Florida, health officials found it infested with 1,200 rats. The only solution, they decided, was to knock the house down. Mrs Parson, 76, who lives with her daughter, said: "To be honest, we didn't notice the rats."
Issue 124: Oct 18th 1997

Maxine and Desmond Quill gave up their bedroom so that their 26 ferrets could move in. They sleep downstairs at their home in Long Eaton, Derbyshire, because their nine cats have the spare room.
Issue 150: April 25th 1998

John Harkins, of Preston, Lancs, swallowed a live goldfish after his friends popped it into his pint as a prank. Harkins had no idea he'd swallowed the fish until he was told. "I'd been feeling queasy anyway," he said, "and I raced to the kitchen to be sick. I brought the fish up and was amazed when it started flapping in the sink. I can't believe it survived, but I bet it was as drunk as I was." The fish made a full recovery.
Issue 175: Oct 17th 1998

An angler whose line got stuck in a bees' nest was chased by the insects along the banks of the Amazon at Rio Negro, Brazil. He finally jumped into the water and was eaten by piranhas.
Issue 176: Oct 24th 1998

In Paisley, Scotland, a pet shop assistant lost his job after he was found juggling the stock. Daniel Hughes, 18, was caught red-handed with three little guinea pigs performing an aerial display.
Issue 182: Nov 28th 1998

A sheep that raised an orphaned elephant as its own has been found dead after the two-year-old elephant sat on her by mistake. The odd pair were inseparable and became national celebrities in South Africa.
Issue 183: Dec 12th 1998

In Cheshire a man has been charged with cruelty to animals. Sean Wilby said he had not intended to hurt Prince, his pet dog, when he accidentally bit him. "Prince and I do a trick together. When I shout 'Oops!' he hurls himself into the air and I catch him in my mouth," he said. "It's not cruel. I do the same with children."
Issue 183: Dec 12th 1998

Jean Fuller was determined to save an injured shrew she found in a hedge. She carried it to her home in Lancashire and was about to give it the kiss of life when she realised it was a teabag.
Issue 190: Feb 6th 1999

Piglet the dog stunned vets when she hobbled into their surgery by herself to get her injured leg treated. The Staffordshire bull terrier was waiting patiently on the doorstep for the first vet to arrive at Crofts Veterinary Practice in Blyth, Northumberland. The hound then went inside and held up her wounded paw. The last time she'd visited the surgery was five years ago. One vet said: "It's absolutely amazing. We can only imagine she remembered us."
Issue 195: March 13th 1999

When Deborah Wilkins found that her pet fish had grown too big for their tank, she ate them. The first to go was a black shark. Then she barbecued an Amazonian pacu, which had grown to two-and-a-half feet, having been imported as a two-inch baby. It was served up to guests with a tangy sauce. "It's wrong," she admitted. "But it was getting far too big. And by eating it, we completed the circle of life. Now, hopefully, its spirit has gone back to the Amazon."
Issue 211: July 3rd 1999

Bob Grice, 50, of Cardiff had to replace a £12.99 library book on disobedient dogs after his dog ate it.
Issue 211: July 3rd 1999

The 50,000 worms which Darlington Football Club bought recently to help irrigate their waterlogged pitch have all drowned.
Issue 217: August 14th 1999

Kennel owner Rita Carlisle of West Bridgeford, Notts, has installed colour TVs so that the dogs in her care can watch their favourite programmes. She said: "If dogs get used to watching the soaps at home, I don't see why they should be deprived of them here."
Issue 216: August 7th 1999

The opening of a new veterinary hospital for sick animals in Izmir, Turkey, was celebrated by the ritual slaughter of a healthy sheep.
Issue 226: Oct 16th 1999

A cat called Turnip is causing a sensation in Atlanta, Georgia, by picking out passages from the Bible on order. Onlookers watch in astonishment as owner Doris Sheiblin bids her pet to locate a passage, naming book, chapter and verse. As witnesses testify, Turnip "listens alertly" then flips to the right page, placing her paw on the exact passage. "Sometimes she gets confused between Nehemiah and Jeremiah," says Doris. "But overall, she gets it right seven out of ten times."
Issue 229: Nov 6th 1999

A man has been arrested for animal cruelty in Paris. Jacques Delhoussy is charged with breaking into 142 pet shops and eating 3,000 canaries.
Issue 237: Jan 8th 2000

A dog which won first prize for "keen intelligence and unquestionable obedience" in a pet show in Shendai, Japan, turned out to be stuffed. "Of course the dog's obedient – it's dead," exclaimed a furious runner-up. But the dog's owner refused to return the £1,000 prize, insisting: "Nobody said the pets had to be alive."
Issue 248: March 25th 2000

An elephant seal is causing chaos in the seaside town of Gisborne, New Zealand, by trying to make love to parked cars. The two-ton creature, named Homer, regularly shuffles out of the ocean to mount the vehicles in a boating-club car park. He is particularly keen on a red Dodge pick-up, but he has also crushed a rubbish bin and two trailers. Witness John Jones said: "Homer is horny and there's not much you can do with an aroused two-ton elephant seal except stand back and admire him."
Issue 252: April 22nd 2000

A hunting dog shot and killed a cat in Gmund, Austria. The dog's owner told police that the shooting occurred as he was packing away his gun outside a local pub. "A cat jumped on the wall and began teasing my dog." The dog, who was stuck in the car, went "mad". When his owner put the gun in the car the dog jumped on the trigger, blasting a hole in the car door, and shot the cat dead. No one is being prosecuted.
Issue 253: April 29th 2000

A jealous cow has been causing havoc for a South African farmer. The cow, Flower, was devoted to Harper Scott, and used to follow him round like a dog. But when he married earlier this year, her mood turned sour. She bellowed angrily whenever she saw the newly-weds holding hands, and once rammed Sarah Scott into a well. "I guess I should get rid of her," said Harper, "but underneath it all she's really a sweetheart."
Issue 256: May 20th 2000

An Alsatian called Gunther has bought Madonna's former home in Miami for £5 million. Gunther, who inherited £100 million from a German countess, signed on the dotted line with a paw print. "Gunther's not stupid with his money," said an aide, explaining why the dog had turned its nose up at Sylvester Stallone's £18 million estate. "He knows a good buy when he sees one." Gunther, who also owns property in Germany, has already made himself at home in Miami. He tours the countryside in a chauffeur-driven BMW and takes occasional dips in his pool.
Issue 265: July 22nd 2000

Computer programmer Sam Maverlin has got into trouble with the people on his street for refusing to get rid of the nine crocodiles which live in his house. Maverlin's neighbours in Los Angeles are now lobbying officials to get the six-foot creatures removed, saying that they live in fear for their lives. Maverlin, however, is unmoved. "My crocs are housebroken," he insists, "and most of them can do simple tricks like rolling over and playing dead. Mostly they just lie around and watch TV or swim in their pool. They even sleep with me at night."
Issue 269: August 19th 2000

A fleet of "enemy submarines" which sparked a major NATO security alert in the Baltic Sea was found to be a shoal of flatulent herrings. Nato officers pressed the alarm button after their hi-tech listening equipment alerted them to rumbles deep in the Baltic. Closer investigation revealed the propeller-like sound to be the noise of farting fish.
Issue 275: Sept 30th 2000

Angler Andy Browne landed a 3ft salmon in a flooded high street in Ringwood, Hampshire. Andy, 39, was walking down the road in his waders when he spotted the 10lb fish darting past traffic lights. He chased it along the street before cornering it in a car park. "I couldn't believe my eyes," he said. "It must be the ultimate fisherman's tale."
Issue 288: Dec 30th 2000

Two animal rights activists were trampled to death by pigs outside a slaughterhouse in Bonn, Germany. They had been protesting about the cruelty of sending pigs to the slaughterhouse when 2,000 of the beasts escaped through a broken fence and stampeded, fatally wounding the protesters in the process.
Issue 288: Dec 30th 2000

A horseman has stunned equestrian fans by training a cow to show-jump. Bruno Isliker, of Oberseen, Switzerland, has already ridden several clear rounds on Sybille the cow, and hopes to put her in for her first competition in Zurich next month.
Issue 294: Feb 17th 2001

A jinxed dog is wreaking havoc in New Zealand. Fluffy keeps having to go back to the Auckland Humane Society because all eight of his owners have died in mysterious circumstances. Director Sean McDougal says: "Every time someone comes in and takes a shine to Fluffy, we warn them about what's happened to his previous owners. But people take one look at his beautiful eyes and just have to take him home. They never think anything bad will happen to them. And they have always been wrong."
Issue 295: Feb 24th 2001

New Zealand farmer Geoff Roder has been banned from his local drive-in cinema for insisting on sitting on the back of a donkey. The 35-year-old bachelor, who is suing the cinema's management, says he took the animal to the movies because it is his only companion, and – since he can't drive – his only means of getting there.
Issue 303: April 21st 2001

A hamster was apprehended after it was seen running along the hard shoulder of the M6 inside a plastic exercise ball. Birmingham motorists saw the hamster weaving along and contacted the RSPCA. It has been christened Roly.
Issue 327: Oct 6th 2001

A square, spotted box-fish called Dotty has fallen in love with one half of a pair of dice. Officials at Bournemouth Oceanarium dropped the die into Dotty's tank hoping it would stop her feeling lonely. "It did the trick," says a spokesman. "Now Dotty won't leave it alone. The two are inseparable."
Issue 334: Nov 24th 2001

An American housewife is offering psychic consultations to troubled pets. Carol Schultz, who claims she can speak the language of animals, charges $50 a session to counsel cats, dogs and horses. Satisfied clients include a dog which was Hitler in a past life and slept all the time to escape depression, and a dog which was trapped in a cat's body.
Issue 341: Jan 19th 2002

Two jet-setting cats have become the first pets to redeem frequent flyer miles from a commercial airline. Babi and Kuukie Rifkin have taken three trips from New York to Israel in the past year, earning them one free flight from El Al's new pet frequent flyer scheme. Their owner says they average four trips a year and love visiting Israel because they were both born there.
Issue 355: April 27th 2002

A parrot suffering from vertigo broke his leg when he fell 80 feet from a tree. George, an African Grey, was perched on a branch outside his Merseyside home when he was struck with a dizzying attack of vertigo. His owner, Janet Rose, tried to coax him down for 24 hours. But when he finally stepped off the branch, he plunged straight to the ground. He is now recovering at home.
Issue 356: May 4th 2002

Spanish inventor Andres Diaz has created the world's first cat-washing machine. The Lavakan, which costs $20,000, has 37 nozzles and three cycles, and can wash a cat in 30 minutes. The animal sits behind a glass door, and disappears behind a wall of water and shampoo, after which the rinse and tumble-dry cycles kick in. "Cats kind of freak out at first," admits Diaz. "Then they calm down."
Issue 358: May 18th 2002

An Australian man got his revenge on a shark that attacked him – by eating it for dinner. Andre Markossian was snorkelling in shallow water when a three-foot shark bit his arm and refused to relinquish its grip. Markossian simply walked to shore with the shark on his arm, where lifeguards pried open its jaws and killed it. Markossian then took the shark home and served his family roasted shark fillets.
Issue 362: June 15th 2002

A farmer in Iowa has bred a herd of miniature cows which he believes will start a new pet craze. Dustin Pillard's herd includes Texas Long-horns, Jerseys and Aberdeen Angus, which are 3ft tall and weigh around 320lb. Pillard claims the creatures, which retail at £600, will make perfect domestic companions.
Issue 366: July 13th 2002

A 17-year-old girl stunned customs officials at Manchester Airport when she walked off a flight wearing a chameleon on her head. The girl, who was travelling from the United Arab Emirates, said she couldn't bear to part with her pet so she pretended it was a hat. Said a fellow passenger: "At first I thought the lizard was plastic, but then I saw its tongue flick out. How the air hostesses did not notice is really beyond me."
Issue 367: July 20th 2002

A wild salmon that had been tagged with a satellite tracking device was logged travelling down the M4. Poachers were delivering it to a restaurant in Wales.
Issue 369: August 3rd 2002

Half a dozen manatees, or sea cows, held an orgy on a Florida beach, swapping partners as beachgoers watched in disbelief. Wildlife specialists were thrilled to witness their sexual frenzy, as manatees are an endangered species, but not everyone was pleased. "Boca Raton is a family community and this public display of sea cow promiscuity has no place here," said one parent.
Issue 374: Sept 7th 2002

Speedy the hamster caused a stir on Blackpool Promenade after whizzing down the pavement in a miniature racing car. Stunned passers-by called the police as the erratically driven dragster sent pedestrians scattering. The car was powered by a treadmill-style hamster wheel, on which Speedy was running furiously. "This is the most unusual case I have ever come across," said PC Quentin Allen, who is trying to trace the animal's owner.
Issue 375: Sept 14th 2002

Australia is to hold its first-ever national sheep-counting championship. Hundreds of sheep will dash past the competitors, who must try to count them. The contestant whose estimate is closest wins. "It sounds like anyone could do it, but it's pretty tough," says contestant Mark Jacka, who regularly counts 60,000 sheep a day in auction yards.
Issue 376: Sept 21st 2002

An Alaskan woman got the surprise of her life when she discovered a black bear using her shower. Suey Linzmeier was working in her garden when she saw the furry beast slip into her house through an open door. "I could hear him wiggling into the shower stall and turning on the water," she said. "After he left the house, I realised he had wiped his face on my husband's bathrobe."
Issue 382: Nov 2nd 2002

A freshly-caught turbot survived 15 hours in a fridge. Mike Reeves caught the fish near his home on the coast of Dorset, wrapped it in foil and placed it in his fridge. When it came time to cook it the next day, he was amazed to find the fish flapping around. "Because it was still alive I didn't have the heart to eat it," said Reeves, who called the local aquarium, which has adopted Herbert and placed him in a tank of salt water.
Issue 384: Nov 16th 2002

A Siamese cat has been freed after a terrifying hostage ordeal. The cat was kidnapped from its owners' front garden in Cosquin, Argentina. The owners received a phone call asking for £100, but the kidnappers eventually settled for £20 and a coffee machine.
Issue 386: Nov 30th 2002

A New Zealand police officer handcuffed a sheep after it attacked his colleague. Two policemen were called out to deal with a loose sheep at a Dunedin farm, but when they arrived the ewe panicked and attacked one of the policemen. The other officer wrestled the sheep to the ground, cuffed its legs together and called for backup. Sergeant Andrew Bardsley said that the sheep is now facing charges of assaulting a police officer.
Issue 387: Dec 7th 2002

A pet shop in Chile has opened a car wash for dogs. Dirty dogs enter a tunnel on a conveyor belt, which takes them through a wash and rinse cycle, then past groomers who do their ears and nails, and finally through a blow-drying tunnel. "We have had an excellent response," said the owner of Dogwash, Javier Fresard, who pipes classical music into the tunnel to help dogs relax. "On hot days we take in around 30 dogs."
Issue 387: Dec 7th 2002

A Dutch sailor who caught a cod was shocked to hear The Ride of the Valkyries emanating from the fish's belly. On filleting the fish, he discovered a Siemens mobile phone in its stomach.
Issue 388: Dec 14th 2002

A four-year-old Indian girl has married a stray dog in a traditional Hindu service. Subal Karmakar said he arranged the bizarre wedding on the advice of an astrologer, who claimed it would cure his daughter Anju of illness. "I did the right thing for my child," he said. "My family has a history of marrying dogs and it always works."
Issue 398: March 1st 2003

The world's first waterskiing squirrel is to make his debut at a boat show in Virginia. Twiggy the squirrel will show off his skills in a 24ft, six-inch-deep pool. Trainer Lou Ann Best has also trained two miniature ponies, two poodles, a toad and an armadillo to water-ski. "It's easy," she says. "You just have to give them a lot of love and affection and tell them the same thing over and over again."
Issue 400: March 15th 2003

Dozens of bulls in Wisconsin have been injured after attempting to mate with a statue of a cow. A farmer placed the shiny cast iron cow in the middle of a pasture to scare off birds, but in the past month almost 50 local bulls have been treated for groin injuries. "I'm currently being sued by several dairy farmers for vet bills," said the farmer.
Issue 401: March 22nd 2003

A veterinary nurse saved a pet snake by giving it the kiss of life. Claire Farina, who works at a surgery in Gloucester, was assisting in an operation when the patient, a Californian king snake called Nipper, stopped breathing. Farina grabbed the 5ft snake, wrenched open its jaws and performed mouth-to-mouth resuscitation. "She saved Nipper's life and I'm so grateful," said the reptile's owner, Ryan Mills.
Issue 405: April 19th 2003

A couple in Minden, Germany, got the fright of their lives when they found a wild boar next to them in bed. The beast, which was being chased by a Yorkshire terrier, had run through the couple's patio door and straight into their bedroom. "I sat up and there was a wild pig in the bed, tusks and everything, trying to hide under the duvet," said Andreas Janik. "I had to hit it on the snout with a newspaper."
Issue 406: April 26th 2003

A dog has been summoned for jury duty in LA. Lucille Marie Gordon, a chocolate labrador, is being threatened with jail after repeatedly failing to turn up for the trial. The dog's owners called the Sacramento Courthouse and explained that Lucille was a dog, but were told: "We've heard every excuse in the book."
Issue 408: May 10th 2003

Police in New Delhi are battling a plague of alcoholic rats. The rats keep breaking into police stations and nibbling into plastic containers full of confiscated moonshine. When drunk, they become fearless and attack the cats that are brought in to kill them. Officials say the rats have also got into their filing cabinets, and are eating vital files on terrorism, murder and corruption cases.
Issue 409: May 17th 2003

Pet shops in Bangkok are doing a roaring trade in illegal African cockroaches. The bugs, which grow up to 2.5 inches long, remain prized possessions despite being banned on health grounds. Officials say they carry germs which can cause inflammation of the brain.
Issue 411: May 31st 2003

An amateur scientist has been eaten alive by a pack of squirrels. Rolf Huber, 34, was attacked in a park in Uelzen, Germany, while testing out an animal repellent. The chemical was intended to make the squirrels flee but instead "it drove them into a murderous rage", said Dr Gerhard Burzle.
Issue 412: June 7th 2003

Australians have taken a new pet to their hearts: the three-inch Australian burrowing cockroach. The creepy-crawlies love humans and hiss with pleasure when stroked. "These are really charming creatures," says a pet shop worker. "They're not stinky at all."
Issue 415: June 28th 2003

San Francisco police had to rescue a floating hen, after it was strapped to 100 helium balloons and sent sailing above the city. Cops popped the balloons with an airgun and the bird floated down into the arms of rescuers. The hen, which has been named Amelia after the aviator Amelia Earhart, is recovering at a shelter until it can find a good home. "This is a great chicken, a friendly chicken, a chicken that is ready for a relationship," says Kat Brown, deputy director of the shelter.
Issue 416: July 5th 2003

Camels in Israel's Negev desert are being fitted with glow-in-the-dark strips to make them more visible to motorists. Officials say that with more than 5,000 camels roaming the desert, they pose a serious traffic hazard. Ten people have been killed and nearly 50 injured in camel-related accidents in the past two years.
Issue 417: July 12th 2003

This year, fashionable dogs are wearing designer shades, says the Daily Mail. The canine sunglasses, which cost up to £85, were designed to protect mountain rescue dogs from snow-blindness, but dog lovers are snapping them up as a fashion accessory. "We found people were prepared to pay a bit more for fashion," says Silvia Wilsch-Herold, head of the German company Dog-goes. "We even do a special gold frame just for Yorkshire terriers".
Issue 421: August 9th 2003

A flock of lazy and disorientated rare birds have been given their own chauffeur-driven car, because they are incapable of migrating by them-selves. Researchers at the Konrad Lorenz centre in Gruenau, Austria, who spent over two years breeding Northern Bald Ibis, have had to drive the birds the 500 miles to their winter quarters in Northern Italy. The stubborn birds, which are about 80cm tall, have got used to the five-star treatment at the research centre and refuse to fly south for the winter.
Issue 426: Sept 13th 2003

Farm animals have been banned from council flats in Kiev, after a survey uncovered 3,000 pigs, 500 cows, 1,000 goats and numerous geese, rabbits and chickens in apartments in the Ukrainian capital. The city authorities say the council buildings were not designed to hold heavy livestock, and that urine from the animals – which were being kept on balconies as well as inside the flats – has been causing structural damage. But residents are furious, saying the animals kept the flats warm in winter.
Issue 429: Oct 4th 2003

A parrot foiled thieves who were ransacking an apartment in Ukraine, after it broke a year of silence and cried out: "Stop, or I'll shoot. On the ground." The bird's owner, an ex-policeman, returned to his flat in Kiev to find three men stretched out on the floor with their hands behind their heads. The parrot had lived with the retired officer for a year but had never spoken before.
Issue 431: Oct 18th 2003

Swedish citizens have been warned to look out for drunk and disorderly elks. The berries on which the animals live have fermented and become alcoholic, making the elks unusually belligerent. Recently, an intoxicated elk was seen chasing a woman through the streets of Karlshamn. "Some elks get calm after they've had alcoholic fruit," says scientist Paul Stamberg, "but others get aggressive, just like humans."
Issue 438: Dec 6th 2003

Scientists have discovered that a common caterpillar can propel its poo five feet through the air – 38 times its own length. Entomologist Martha Weiss was amazed when she saw the silver-spotted skipper larva let fly at 4.2ft a second. "One moment a pellet is there, the next it's gone," says Weiss, who believes the creatures developed the talent in order to keep their nests tidy.
Issue 440: Dec 20th 2003

An elderly elephant in Thailand is enjoying a new lease of life after being fitted with a set of custom-made false teeth. Morakot, who lives in captivity at a park in Kanchanaburi, couldn't chew her food because she had lost all her teeth. The 80-year-old elephant had become so weak that she had to be supported by a sling hung from a tree. The zoo vet, Dr Somsak Jitniyom, made her a huge set of dentures from stainless steel and plastic, and Morakot is now happily tucking into her food once again.
Issue 443: Jan 17th 2004

Blu Cantrell spares no expense when it comes to her pet, says the Daily Mirror. The singer spends £10,000 a month on her dog, Pepper, including £3,000 for a live-in nanny. Pepper also wears a £50,000 diamond-encrusted collar. "She's like my daughter," says Blu. "She's my safe way of having a child. The other way would make me fat and bloated and hinder my career."
Issue 443: Jan 17th 2004

A woman who brought her cat into a vet's surgery killed five birds in the waiting room when she took off her shoes. Her feet were so smelly that they asphyxiated two cockatiels and three parakeets, and the vet's office had to be closed temporarily by order of the Department of Public Health. "The odour was horrendous," said receptionist Maria Ferrara.
Issue 444: Jan 24th 2004

Luke Tresoglavic was swimming near Newcastle, Australia, when a wobbegong shark sank its teeth into his leg and refused to let go. Tresoglavic, 22, swam 1,000ft to the shore, got into his car and drove to his surf club with the creature still stuck to his leg. "Could you get this thing off?" he asked the club's lifeguards, who forced the 2ft shark to loosen its grip by hosing it with fresh water. "There was an element of humour to it," says the surfer, who was left with 70 needle-like punctures.
Issue 448: Feb 21st 2004

Three livestock exhibitors have been disqualified from Ohio State Fair for using hairpieces on their cows. Scott Long and brothers Kreg and Kenneth Krebs glued fake hair on to their Holstein cattle to make their backs look straighter. The toupees were discovered when inspectors ran their hands over the cows to check for any illegal grooming tricks.
Issue 448: Feb 21st 2004

A man who created a reptile-and-insect zoo in his flat was killed by Bettina, his favourite black widow spider, and then eaten by his other pets. Police in Dortmund, Germany, broke into Mark Voegel's flat after neighbours reported a horrid smell. They found the 30-year-old loner dead on the sofa, covered in giant cobwebs, while 200 spiders, several snakes, thousands of termites and a lizard called Helmut munched on his corpse. "It was like a horror movie," reported one of the officers at the scene.
Issue 450: March 6th 2004

A German artist has written to zoos all over the country asking if they would be prepared to feed his body to piranhas after he dies. Karl Friedrich Lentze, 56, hopes that the spectacle will be his final contribution to art. "It's a great idea," says Günther Nogge, director of Cologne Zoo. "But it would be better if you were fed to the piranhas alive: they're not keen on dead flesh." "They could always poke my body with sticks to get me moving and get the fish interested," says Lentze.
Issue 454: April 3rd 2004

A bull that pined for its late owner has been led away from his grave after a two-day vigil. The bull, called Barnaby, escaped from his field in the German town of Roedental and jumped over a wall to get into the cemetery a mile down the road, where Alfred Gruenemeyer was buried. The eccentric farmer is said to have treated his animals like pets, giving them the run of his home.
Issue 456: April 17th 2004

A pensioner was saved from an alligator attack by her fearless husband. Jane Keefer, 74, was working in her garden in Sanibel, Florida, when the ten-foot beast lunged at her and dragged her into a nearby lagoon. Her husband William, 78, dived into the water and wrestled the alligator's jaws open. The creature was later captured and destroyed.
Issue 458: May 1st 2004

A Chinese businessman claims to have swatted eight million flies in ten years. Hu Xilin began killing flies after one landed in a client's meal during a work lunch – costing him a £13,000 deal. Hu, from Zhejiang, vowed revenge. He has since devised several fly-killing contraptions and spent £20,000 hiring a "swat" team to help him wipe out the insects.
Issue 464: June 6th 2004

A tiny Mexican village has elected a mule as its mayor. "The previous mayor had been arrested for bribery and so had the chief of police," said Elian Santiago, a resident of Mesa Blanco. "One day in church our priest said it would be better to have an honest donkey than a dishonest man." The town rallied behind a mule named Pickles, who defeated two other candidates by 80 votes. "Everyone in town trusts Señor Pickles," says Santiago. "He is known for his honesty and good nature.
Issue 466: June 26th 2004

An Iranian woman has given birth to a frog with human characteristics. The Iranian newspaper Etemaad says the creature is thought to have grown from spawn to an adult frog inside the woman's body. Doctors in the south-eastern city of Iranshahr say she could have picked up the spawn unknowingly while swimming in a dirty pool. The frog has yet to undergo tests but experts claim it looks faintly human.
"The similarities are in the shape of the fingers and the size and shape of the tongue," says biologist Dr Aminifard.
Issue 467: July 3rd 2004

A Brazilian congressman is trying to make it illegal for animals to be given human names. Reinaldo Santos e Silva is concerned that children will get depressed if they discover that they share their first name with someone's pet.
Issue 486: Nov 13th 2004

A two-headed tortoise has been hatched in Dorset. "I had never seen anything like it," said John Jones, 66, who bred the reptile. Named Solomon and Sheba because its sex is unknown, the tortoise is in good health, and has a healthy appetite. "Both heads eat at the same time. Sometimes they start on the same bit of food and meet in the middle."
Issue 487: Nov 20th 2004

A Bulgarian farmer is demanding compensation from the dealer who sold him a homosexual pedigree pig. Galen Dobrev says the 220lb boar's sexual preferences became apparent as soon as he got it home. "It was a disgrace," he told the court. "All it was interested in was other male pigs." No one would buy the pig, and in the end, he had to turn it into sausages.
Issue 488: Nov 27th 2004

Zookeepers at a wildlife park in Kent are learning French to help them communicate with a new group of guinea baboons from Paris. "We shout, 'allez allez allez', which always seems to get them about," said keeper Mike Downman. "And when I walk into the enclosure I say things like 'Bon matin'. I think it's helped them settle in."
Issue 496: Jan 29th 2005

Elephants in Thailand have been taught to keep the jungle clean by using their own custom-built lavatory. The tuskers not only sit on the giant convenience, they also flush it, by pulling on a dangling cord. The owners of the Palaad Tawanron camp near Chiang Mai then use the waste to produce methane gas.
Issue 496: Jan 29th 2005

An Oklahoma senator hopes to revive cockfighting by putting tiny boxing gloves on roosters. Cockfighting was banned in Oklahoma in 2002, but Sen. Frank Shurden plans to appease animal rights activists by making the roosters wear gloves over their spurs and vests with sensors to record hits. "It's like fencing," he says. "Who's going to object to chickens fighting like humans?"
Issue 497: Feb 5th 2005

Frozen chickens have been falling from the sky in Newcastle, Australia, baffling the authorities. The projectiles have damaged several homes, in some cases plunging straight through the roof. "Frozen chickens hurtling through the stratosphere is just one of the mysteries of existence," said New South Wales premier Bob Carr. "I can't explain it."
Issue 500: Feb 26th 2005

A taxidermist from Nevada has found a novel way for animal lovers to remember the deceased: pet pillows. Jeanette Hall, 29, says she has already sold hundreds of cushions made from the pelts of dead pets. The cost is £35 for a small cat cushion, or £80 for a large dog.
Issue 506: April 9th 2005

A ram caused £10,000 worth of damage to a row of brand new cars by attacking his reflection in the gleaming bodywork. Rambo the ram repeatedly butted the six Land Rovers and Mitsubishi Shoguns, thinking he was facing a love rival. The cars had been parked in a field in Haverfordwest, Wales, because there was not enough room at the local garage. At first, garage boss Martin Green thought vandals were to blame. But when his mechanic, Claude Brevost, went to collect one of the cars, Rambo charged at him too. "Claude was a bit bruised," said Green, "but at least it solved the mystery."
Issue 508: April 23rd 2005

Hamburg has been hit by an epidemic of exploding toads. Thousands of the creatures have been spotted swelling up to four times their original size and then bursting, sending entrails several feet into the air. Zoologists have declared themselves baffled as to both the cause and the location. "You see the toads crawling along the ground, swelling until they are like little tennis balls – and then they suddenly explode," said an animal protection worker.
Issue 509: April 30th 2005

When a dark cloud suddenly appeared over their village in rural Serbia, and hundreds of frogs fell from the sky, the locals came up with two possible explanations: either a plane carrying crate loads of amphibians had exploded as it passed overhead, or the world was coming to an end. Fortunately, a climate expert was able to put their fears to rest with a less apocalyptic analysis: "A whirlwind had sucked up the frogs from a lake and carried them along to Odzaci where they fell to the ground," said Slavisa Ignjatovic. "It is a recognised scientific phenomenon."
Issue 515: June 11th 2005

A Chinese man pretended to be a hunchback so he could smuggle his pet turtle on to an aeroplane. Mr Wu, who was travelling to Chongqing, strapped the turtle to his back and walked through security before being stopped by a guard who thought his hump looked suspicious. Wu, who is in his sixties, apologised for smuggling the animal but said he couldn't bear to leave his pet behind.
Issue 511: May 14th 2005

A Romanian farmer is hoping to make a fortune after a four-legged chick was born on his farm. The chick is perfectly healthy, and Doru Grigoras is hoping she will produce an entire line of four-legged offspring when she grows up. "Think of all the extra chicken drumsticks you can get," he said.
Issue 516: June 18th 2005

A woman in Dubai was attacked by a four-foot-long python as she watched a film at her local cinema. The woman began screaming hysterically when she felt something slithering up her leg. "Someone with a mobile phone with a flashlight pointed at it, and we saw it was a snake," said fellow cinemagoer Sherana Alansudhir. "I told her to shut up and stop screaming. It was curling up tighter on her leg. So I got hold of the snake's tail, unwrapped the snake and carried it to the foyer."
Issue 517: June 25th 2005

A 500lb brown bear has been terrifying rural Croatians by knocking on their doors and raiding their kitchens. The bear has learnt that knocking is the easiest way to gain entry to a house. "I opened the door and saw him standing there," said Nevenka Loknar. "He walked in as if it was the most natural thing in the world." After two further raids, the Loknar family have stopped answering the door.
Issue 521: July 23rd 2005

A Californian air-quality watchdog has ordered farmers to get their flatulent cows under control. The farting and burping of 2.5 million local cows has been blamed for the smog problem in the San Joaquin Valley. Farmers have been told to install anti-pollution technology and change the cows' diets to reduce their production of natural methane. "We are talking about a public health crisis," says a spokesman for the environment lobby group. "It's not funny to joke about cow burps and farts when one in six children in Fresno is carrying an inhaler."
Issue 524: August 6th 2005

Squirrels in Brixton may be becoming addicted to crack cocaine. The creatures, which have a powerful sense of smell, are said to have got hooked on crack after digging up stashes hidden by dealers in front gardens. Residents in the south London borough have reported seeing them scrabbling about, searching for more. "They hang out in the little park in front of the Ritzy, twitching… dancing to music only they can hear and generally creating a malevolent ambience," wrote one London blogger.
Issue 533: Oct 15th 2005

A woman from Redbridge in East London has married a dolphin. The dolphin, Cindy, swam to the edge of his enclosure for the ceremony in Eliat, Israel, to join bride Sharon Tendler, who wore a white silk dress and a pink tiara. After the ceremony, Miss Tendler kissed Cindy and whispered "I love you" into his blow hole, before diving into the water in her dress for a hug. "Cindy is 35 and I've been visiting him on holidays for 15 years," said Miss Tendler. "He's lovely."
Issue 544: Jan 7th 2006

A man in Austria lost more than he bargained for while playing cards, when his friend's dog chewed off his toe during a game. Gottfried Fischler, 61, from St Andra in Carinthia, is paralysed from the waist down so he did not feel a thing. "It was only when a player saw the blood that I realised," said Mr Fischler. "The dog must have been hungry – I've not got the nicest feet in the world."
Issue 545: Jan 14th 2006

A three-year-old budgie has been voted Young Cross-Stitcher of the Year, reports The Sun. The bird, Spike, used to sit on her owner's shoulder as she did her sewing. "One day I just sat and didn't stitch. It seemed to frustrate her," said Sandra Battye, 31. "Then suddenly she picked up the needle in her beak and began cross-stitching herself. Now I can't stop her. She gets confused at how the patterns work but she is very good at pulling and pushing the needle through the fabric."
Issue 547: Jan 28th 2006

French farmers are offering British gastronomes their own herd of snails. For £22, buyers get 120 snails, which they can watch online from "birth to boiling water". The snails will then be shelled and sent in a jar to their owners.
Issue 547: Jan 28th 2006

A dachshund in Austria has made it to the ripe old age of 22, despite a lifelong addiction to cigarettes. Owner Wolfgang Treitler says General Edi is "as fit as a puppy" and attributes his longevity to the ten cigarettes he has eaten every day for 17 years. "He eats the tobacco and the paper, and then chews a while on the filter before spitting it out."
Issue 550: Feb 18th 2005

Celebrities Challenged

Ruth Kensit, 21, the younger sister of Patsy Kensit, is dating Sir Clive Sinclair, aged 54. She keeps him happy by declining to wear bra and pants when they go out on the town together. "His car may have been a flop, says the underwear spurning actress, "but Sir Clive certainly isn't."
Issue 4: June 17th 1995

"My Tortoise Left Me Scarred For Life!" said a headline in the News of the World magazine. Catherine Zeta-Jones, the star of The Darling Buds of May, came close to death as a baby after catching a virus from her pet tortoise. A blockage had to be removed from her throat leaving a scar which is still visible.
Issue 10: July 19th 1995

Mel Gibson on the film set of Braveheart asked a Scots extra what was under his kilt. The dour reply was "Your wife's lipstick." Gibson says: "I didn't know whether to hug him or hit him."
Issue 17: Sept 16th 1995

Supermodel Cindy Crawford ordered a props man on the set of her first movie to write out 100 times "I must not call Cindy fat" after he teased her about her weight.
Issue 33: Jan 13th 1996

In a fax to John Kennedy Jnr., George Clooney wrote: "Congratulations on your wedding – and thanks for passing the torch to me as America's No 1 bachelor."
Issue 73: Oct 19th 1996

Sharon Stone dumped her French boyfriend Michael Benastra after he broke his diet while they were holidaying in Morocco. After flushing his lamb stew down the loo, she screamed: "As soon as we get back to LA I'm going to see that your belly is liposuctioned off." Michael said he was sick and tired of her trying to starve him to death.
Issue 77: Nov 16th 1996

Julia Roberts is still recovering from the moment she met her co-star, Mel Gibson, on the set of Conspiracy Theory. Gibson gave her a large, exquisitely wrapped parcel. Inside was a freeze-dried rat.
Issue 80: Dec 7th 1996

Jamie Lee Curtis had the script of the film Fierce Creatures rewritten so that her breasts could be more exposed. "My chest has a world of it's own," she explained. "It has an agent, a publicist, a fan club, a web page. There's a whole city out there devoted to these breasts."
Issue 87: Feb 1st 1997

Rock star Prince has explained why he turned down the offer to star in Michael Jackson's video, Bad. "The first line in the song is 'Your butt is mine'. I said to Michael, 'Whose going to sing that to who ? Because you sure ain't singing that to me, and I sure ain't singing that to you.' So from there we had a problem."
Issue 88: Feb 8th 1997

Actor Brad Pitt buys a bicycle every time he visits a new city and then leaves it locked to a lamppost ready for when he visits again. "The wheels are usually missing when I get back," he says.
Issue 106: June 14th 1997

Madonna ditched her lover Carlos Leon when he failed to "satisfy her demands for sex" according to The Sun. The singer made the fitness trainer carry a pager so she could track him down when she wanted to make love. Carlos told a friend, "when she wants it, I'm supposed to drop everything and go round and service her. It got very tiresome."
Issue 100: July 12th 1997

Fourteen-year-old actor Taylor Jones asked Al Pacino how he got so many gorgeous women. Pacino replied: "I say to them, 'You tired?' They say, 'No, why?' I say, 'Because you've been running around my mind all day.'"
Issue 111: July 19th

The actress Cher so hated her suite's wallpaper at Cannes' exclusive Hotel Du Cap that she demanded the staff temporarily staple a new design on top.
Issue 117: August 30th 1997

When Michael Douglas saw that Jack Nicholson had come to witness him leaving his handprint on Hollywood's Walk of Fame, he told the fellow actor he was honoured he was there. "Don't be," replied Nicholson. "I just came to see you where you belong – on your knees."
Issue 126: Nov 1st 1997

Status Quo's Rick Parfitt needs to get out more, according to the News of the World. The Status Quo star recently confided; "Before my heart problem I didn't drink tea. Now it's one cup after another. Always use a teabag twice, and over 20 years you'll save £19 – I worked that out."
Issue 130: Nov 29th 1997

Barbara Streisand's romance with Pierre Trudeau, former president of Canada, was doomed from the start. "Trudeau was a man I wasn't ready for," the singer told the Evening Standard. "In other words, he was magnificent. It scared me, even though my lucky number is 24 and he lived at 24 Sussex Drive."
Issue 133: Dec 20th 1997

Big Breakfast presenter Denise Van Outen, 23, shocked guests at a Caribbean hotel by walking around in her bra, G-string and woolly Rasta hat. Later, she went out to her balcony, pulled up her skirt and showed her knickers to passers-by, yelling: "Hey Bahamas, check out my growler."
Issue 135: Jan 10th 1998

When police stopped a speeding Mercedes at 5.30am, they failed to recognise Posh Spice Victoria Adams at the wheel. The usually immaculate Spice Girl was dressed in shorts and a sweatshirt, her hair tied up with a pair of knickers. Posh pleaded: "Look, I'm a Spice Girl and I'm late for work." They let her off.
Issue 136: Jan 17th 1998

Actor Matt Dillon has put 150lbs of metal under his bed to ensure that he doesn't father a "demon" child. Dillon, who is dating actress Cameron Diaz, consulted a Feng Shui expert on how to get the most positive energy out of his home. When they reached the master bedroom, the Chinese specialist exclaimed: "It's no good! You may have baby. Baby be demon seed." Dillon immediately installed a slab of metal under the bed to "neutralise that energy". He told talk-show host Jay Leno: "I look at it as an insurance policy."
Issue 139: Feb 7th 1998

Jerry Springer, host of the eponymous US chat show, claims that the impotency pill Viagra has turned him into a sex addict. Springer was recently discovered in a steamy clinch with porn star Kendra Jade, who was to appear on his show. "That damned Viagra made me lose my mind," he told a friend. "I thought I was some kind of sexual superman."
Issue 154: May 23rd 1998

Tara Palmer-Tomkinson was snapped by paparazzi while frolicking topless in Los Angeles recently. But the It Girl remains sanguine. My chest "must be the smallest one ever to appear on Page Three", she wrote in The Sunday Times. I was just trying to "take advantage of the sun… In the end, it was The Sun that took advantage of me."
Issue 146: March 28th 1998

Hollywood couple Jim Carrey and Lauren Holly have made a love pact in a bid to save their marriage. They have agreed to sleep together only once a week so that Jim can prove his desire to be with her is not just based on lust. The star of The Mask also had to vow to stop making funny faces every time he passes a mirror, as his facial antics were infuriating his wife.
Issue 153: May 16th 1998

Sonny Bono's grave has failed to match the expectations of his former wife, Cher. After visiting his resting place in Palm Springs cemetery, the singer declared that it did not "reflect the fun and excitement he generated in life", and that she is hoping to get a more fitting headstone erected. "A pinball machine or something like that," she mused. "Sonny would dig it."
Issue 159: June 27th

Sylvester Stallone has called his new baby daughter Sistine, after the Vatican chapel. He had wanted to call her Incontinence, because, as he explained, "it means spanning all continents". The word he was actually looking for, said his wife, Jennifer Flavin, was Intercontinental.
Issue 162: July 18th 1998

Leonardo DiCaprio looked so pale and gaunt while strolling along a beach north of Malibu, California, that an old lady took a home-made sandwich out of her bag and handed it to the actor. He thanked her, adding, "You know I'm actually a big move star." The old lady, walking away, said: "Yeah, and I'm Raquel Welch. Enjoy."
Issue 163: July 25th 1998

When Jack Nicholson, 51, spotted a pretty blonde in a London street, he stopped to invite her to a party. "I'm great at it," he told her. She declined his invitation. "Don't you recognise me?" he asked. "Yes, you're Charles Bronson and you look much older and wrinklier without your wig," she replied. Nicholson was stunned: Bronson is 83.
Issue 163: July 25th 1998

Sir Clive Sinclair's latest love is former Miss England Angie Bowness, a lap-dancer aged 21. "Clive has proposed many times," she said. "And I'm considering saying yes." This is news to Mark Thornton, father of her three-month-old child. "I feel shocked and humiliated," he stormed. "How can a gorgeous woman like that even consider this balding old man?" Angie's mother, however, likes the 57-year-old inventor: "Sir Clive comes to see us quite often," she beamed. "He is very intellectually stimulating."
Issue 164: August 1st 1998

Baywatch star Yasmine Bleeth has confessed that she has sexual fantasies about supermodel Cindy Crawford. "I'm obsessed with Cindy," she admitted. "There is something about her, something enchanting, voluptuous. Cindy and Elvis would be my perfect threesome."
Issue 165: August 8th 1998

Supermodel Caprice has revealed that she washes her hair in tomato ketchup. The bottle-blonde former Wonderbra girl said: "The chlorine in swimming pools turns my hair green, but tomato ketchup stops that."
Issue 171: Sept 19th 1998

Chris Eubank has been having an affair with a young fan for six years, says the News of the World. The boxer seduced star-struck virgin Zoey Avis after she asked for his autograph. In bed, Avis says, Eubank "was like a proud animal, showing off his flawless, sculptured body... His favourite position was making love to me when he could see himself in the mirror." And he would always keep his white socks on. Zoey, now a 24-year-old model, dumped the married former champion last week after deciding she wanted more out of life than "sex in hotel rooms".
Issue 172: Sept 26th 1988

Kate Moss was bemused when she met Jeremy Clarkson at a showbiz party. The TV presenter introduced himself with a cheery: "Hi, I'm Jeremy Clarkson, I do Top Gear." "'Ere!" replied Kate, wrinkling her nose. "Are you trying to sell me drugs?"
Issue 174: Oct 10th 1998

Steve Tyler, lead singer with the rock group Aerosmith, wants his ashes scattered over a beach full of scantily clad beauties: "I still want to be able to get into girls' pants when I'm dead," he explained.
Issue 176: Oct 24th 1998

Bret Michaels, Pamela Anderson's former lover, has revealed intimate details of their "kinky affair" two years ago. Bret, lead singer with the rock group Poison, said Pamela liked to dress up as a virgin while he made love to her in a Dracula costume. She also liked having hot wax dripped on to her and frequently stripped off her clothes and drove his BMW at 100mph while he caressed her.
Issue 177: Oct 31st 1998

Page Three model Katie "Jordan" Price – dubbed "The Girl for the Thrillennium" – has topless modelling in her blood. "My family have always been very open-minded," she told Loaded magazine. "Even my nan. In her day she was a topless mermaid in a tank. Men used to look at her through a kind of telescope. But she got the sack for smoking on the job. She had massive tits, my nan."
Issue 185: Jan 2nd 1999

Sylvester Stallone splashed out £26,000 this Christmas on breast implants to "boost the assets" of his wife Jennifer Flavin, her sister Trish and two of Jennifer's closest friends. A friend said: "I know it sounds strange, but it's important for Sly that the women in his life look good."
Issue 186: Jan 9th 1999

Cameron Diaz has agreed to take her unfaithful boyfriend Matt Dillon back – at a price. The actress is demanding that Dillon puts £500,000 in a special account to ensure he keeps his promise to stay faithful. If he strays he loses both her and the cash, which will be given to charity.
Issue 188: Jan 23rd 1999

Pop Star Mariah Carey was one of the first celebrities to comment on the death of King Hussein of Jordan. "I'm inconsolable," Carey told CNN. "I was a very good friend of Jordan. He was probably the greatest basketball player this country has ever seen. We will never see his like again." The singer was informed that it wasn't Michael Jordan who had died, before being led off by her bodyguards "in a state of confusion".
Issue 192: Feb 20th 1998

David Duchovny is taking his responsibilities as a father-to-be seriously. The X Files star wears a strap-on plastic "empathy belly" around the house so he can share the pregnancy experience with his girlfriend, Tea Leoni.
Issue 192: Feb 20th 1998

Barbra Streisand is so scared of the Millennium Bug that she has backed out of a New Year's Eve concert for which she was to be paid $10 million and is turning her home into a fortress. "Planes could crash, electricity and water supplies could fail, mobs may roam the streets burning and pillaging," she told a friend. She plans to employ armed guards to patrol her house. "I want a whole team of hunks keeping me safe."
Issue 193: Feb 27th 1999

Elizabeth Hurley has a secret for keeping thin, reports the National Enquirer: the model brings a miniature set of knives and forks to restaurants to help her eat smaller portions.
Issue 195: March 13th 1999

A man almost died after seeing Barbara Windsor without her clothes on. PR man Simon Porter was with the EastEnders star as she changed for a photoshoot. Windsor joked: "An ageing sex symbol half-naked in front of you. You'll have a heart attack if you're not careful." At which point, Porter was rushed to hospital suffering from palpitations. "I'll make sure she keeps her clothes on in front of me from now on," he told The Sun.
Issue 196: March 20th 1999

Former Spice Girl Geri Halliwell thinks she knows why she hasn't got a man. "I don't shave my legs. I haven't got really hairy legs and I think spiky stubble is worse." Her bedtime habits may also be an obstacle. "I go to sleep with my make-up on and things like that," she admits. But the singer isn't overly fussy: her ideal mate is "rounded and with beer breath".
Issue 198: April 3rd 1999

Jennifer Aniston's recent attempt to boost her bosom went badly wrong, reports the National Enquirer. The Friends star put water-filled pads in her bra for a night out at an LA restaurant. But she fled in panic after a friend accidentally punctured them with a chopstick. "It was an amazing sight to see this famous actress with water coming out of her boobs," said a waiter.
Issue 200: April 17th 1999

The singer Celine Dion escapes fans who hover backstage at her gigs by hiding in a suitcase. "She just crouches inside the case then her roadies wheel her from her dressing room to the stage," said a friend. "None of the fans ever suspect their idol is going right past their noses."
Issue 203: May 8th 1999

Hugh Grant has admitted to a childhood passion for Cliff Richard. "I had a crush on him for the longest time," says Grant. "That means I had bad musical taste and that I was gay, presumably."
Issue 206: May 29th 1999

Ace, star of ITV's Gladiators, has ditched Page 3 girl Jordan because he couldn't cope with her kinky tastes. Ace told the Sunday People he was scared "witless" when she first took him to her bedroom: "There were whip marks on the walls and the wardrobe was bursting with kinky PVC outfits and the draws were stuffed with peek-a-boo bras...When she showed me her handcuffs, I thought it was just a bit of a joke. But when she cracked a giant bullwhip on the floor and said, 'Who's been a naughty boy then?' I realised she was deadly serious."
Issue 209: June 19th 1999

Actress Heather Graham did not relish the prospect of having to kiss her co-star in Austin Powers: The Spy Who Shagged Me. "Mike Myers was very hairy and had all these horrible teeth that stuck out," she told the News of the World. "So I ate tuna casserole with extra onions and garlic to speed up his kissing a bit."
Issue 211: July 3rd 1999

Jo Wood, wife of the Rolling Stone Ronnie Wood, was thrilled to meet Ian Hislop at a recent party. When he introduced himself as the editor of Private Eye magazine, she chirped: "Oh, we need a private eye. Someone keeps stealing our pot plants."
Issue 212: July 10th 1999

Ex-Spice Girl Geri Halliwell likes to get the red carpet treatment wherever she goes – so she brings her own. On a recent promotional visit to an LA record store her driver produced a red carpet from the trunk of the car and rolled it out for her.
Issue 215: July 31st 1999

Diana Rigg has been voted the sexiest TV star of all time by America's TV Guide. The 60-year-old Avengers star said: "Sometimes I see pictures of myself and I think, 'God, I was really quite tasty.' I didn't know it at the time." But she's not convinced she deserves the current adulation: "I am deeply honoured but a bit confused. I was only ever a B-cup."
Issue 217: August 14th 1999

Hugh Grant has admitted to beating up a German driver in a road-rage row, reports the Daily Star. The actor angered the motorist by stepping out in front of his car, forcing him to brake. "This chap started slapping me about," said Grant. "I tried saying 'steady on old boy', but he was in a blind rage. When that failed I'm afraid I lost my temper and whacked him quite hard on the nose. It knocked his little German hat off."
Issue 219: August 28th 1999

Helena Bonham-Carter claims that she is not as refined as her name suggests. "People imagine I'm so cultured. The truth is I drink a lot of diet coke, tell dirty jokes and arm wrestle," insists the actress. "A double-barrelled surname merely makes it hell signing autographs."
Issue 221: Sept 11th 1999

David Bowie enjoys travelling on the London Underground. To avoid being spotted he goes disguised in a hat and glasses and carries a Greet newspaper.
Issue 223: Sept 25th 1999

According to The Mirror, when David Beckham was asked to write a cheque to Customs and Excise, he made it out for "Costumes and Exercise" instead. The footballer explained that he "thought it was for [his wife] Victoria's health club".
Issue 227: Oct 23rd 1999

Jack Nicholson, eating out in an LA restaurant with his latest flame, Twin Peaks star Lara Flynn Boyle, was furious when a flower seller approached his table and asked: "How about flowers for your grand-daughter?" Jack was about to let out a stream of abuse when he spotted Danny DeVito chuckling in the corner. Danny had paid the woman $20 to embarrass his fellow actor.
Issue 227: Oct 23rd 1999

John Travolta has decided to call his new child Spam because pregnant wife Kelly Preston, 36, has cravings for the reconstituted meat and keeps a tin in the bedroom for a midnight snack. Spam, due next spring, will provide company for the actor's son Jett, who was named after Travolta's love of flying.
Issue 228: Oct 30th 1999

Demi Moore has taken to holding "intuition" sessions at her home in which she burns anything she thinks is making her life miserable, reports The Mirror. At the latest meeting she flung a red and blue tie into her living room fireplace, saying: "Last night I asked myself, 'what is in my way? What is holding me back?' For some reason it was a man's tie. The tie symbolises, for me, the choking off of my life."
Issue 230: Nov 13th 1999

Friends star Matthew Perry was dumped by his live-in lover Rene after she found a "huge black bra" in their bed. Rene, 29, told the National Enquirer: "I'd tolerated his flirting and drinking. But when I found a bra that was three sizes too big for me I knew he'd been cheating. He couldn't even come up with a decent lie. He said he had no idea how the bra got into our bed. He even had the nerve to try to convince me it was mine."
Issue 236: Dec 25th 1999

Heavy-rockers Aerosmith have revealed the secret of their longevity: spinach. The famously dissolute rock stars, who have confessed to spending over £10m on drugs over the years, are hooked on spinach washed down with camomile tea. "We have our spinach, that's why we're still here," says the band's front man Steve Tyler.
Issue 237: Jan 8th 2000

Angelina Jolie has been voted the actress most men – and women – would like to sleep with. "It's probably because I'm probably the one actress who'd say yes," she told the Daily Star. Angelina has a reputation for extreme behaviour. Her hobby is collecting knives, she eats nothing but red meat and her childhood ambition was to be a funeral director. When she married British actor Jonny Lee Miller, she wrote his name across her white silk blouse in her own blood.
Issue 239: Jan 22nd 2000

Sigourney Weaver has married off her pet dog, reports the News of the World. The bride wore an elaborate wedding dress, while the groom sported a bow tie. "My greyhound met a very handsome Italian greyhound and we had to marry her," said the actress. "She had a beautiful wedding dress and my daughter was minister. We had dog vows and a cake. It's so romantic."
Issue 241: Feb 5th 2000

When Elizabeth Taylor's poodle, Sugar, chipped his tooth on a biscuit, she rushed him off to a Beverly Hills dentist to have it capped. The actress was so pleased with the result that she is now spending £9,500 on having the rest of his teeth fixed.
Issue 242: Feb 12th 2000

Barbra Streisand takes no chances. The diva sent an assistant down to the Golden Globe ballroom, days before the awards ceremony, to take photographs from all angles so that she could decide exactly where she should sit to look her best when accepting her lifetime achievement award.
Issue 244: Feb 26th 2000

Cybill Shepherd is no wallflower when it comes to men. In her autobiography, the actress boasts a roll call of sleeping partners including Elvis Presley, Don Johnson, a 17-year-old toy boy and two stuntmen (at once).
Issue 246: March 11th 2000

Rod Stewart's estranged wife Rachel Hunter has announced that she is desperate for a lover. "I need a stallion. I want to make the most of my Dirty Thirties," the model declared. "I am revved up and ready to go. Women can be a right pain if they're not getting it, and I haven't had it for seven months."
Issue 248: March 25th 2000

Sales of Brylcreem have plunged 25 per cent since David Beckham, who has a contract to promote the product, had his head shaved. Tesco is slashing prices on the hair cream in an attempt to restore sales.
Issue 249: April 1st 2000

Bjork's reputation for eccentricity is well deserved, says The Express. During the filming of Dancer in the Dark, the Icelandic singer-turned-actress stormed off the set so often that its director, Lars Von Trier, smashed two TV sets in frustration. When he asked her to wear a costume she disliked, she ripped it into tiny pieces and ate it.
Issue 257: May 27th 2000

Michael Jackson refused to attend Elizabeth Taylor's tribute at the Royal Albert Hall until a team of 27 security guards had been assembled to shadow his every move. Jackson also demanded that the seating in his box was covered with plastic sheeting and an air purifying system was fitted to ward off any germs from the 2,000-strong crowd.
Issue 258: June 3rd 2000

No beauty regime is too arduous for Liz Hurley, reports the National Enquirer. The model and actress makes her assistant sandpaper her bottom when she gets out of the bath, to keep it nice and smooth. Hurley also carries an oxygen inhaler with her at all times, and takes regular shots to keep her pores from clogging.
Issue 263: July 8th 2000

Robbie Williams broke up with his former girlfriend, All Saints singer Nicole Appleton, because he couldn't meet her insatiable sexual appetite, claims the News of the World. After a particularly gruelling weekend, Robbie told a friend: "I'm not sure I can cope any more. She had me every way possible. She wouldn't even let me out to get a pint of milk."
Issue 262: July 1st 2000

Melanie Sykes is something of a maneater, according to Maxim. "I mentally undress blokes all the time," confessed the t.v. presenter. "I keep doing double takes to check the rear." She isn't keen on men dressing up in the bedroom – "naked's the best way" – with one exception. "I find firemen very attractive. It's such a macho job."
Issue 264: July 15th 2000

Winona Ryder's love life hasn't really recovered since her break-up with Matt Damon. The actress claims she has resorted to dating herself. "I'm taking myself out to dinner," said the 29-year-old, "and I may end up taking advantage of myself. Maybe I'll even tie myself up."
Issue 265: July 22nd 2000

Macauley Culkin, once Hollywood's highest-paid child star, has turned into a miserable couch potato, says the National Enquirer. The 19-year-old actor recently separated from his wife, Rachel, who is fed up with his slovenly ways. "He does nothing but lie around watching wrestling on TV," she claims. Culkin also smokes incessantly. "He smokes when he watches wrestling, he smokes when he plays video games. All he does is smoke," says Rachel. He even had a cigarette in his hand when the couple walked down the aisle two years ago. "Someone had to pry the cigarette from his fingers," says a family friend.
Issue 272: Sept 9th 2000

Scary Spice Mel B insisted on snogging her fellow Spice Girls after having her tongue pierced because she was worried that her kissing skills might have been impaired by the operation. "I wanted to know what it felt like to have a snog with a pierced tongue," said the singer. "The girls all said it felt all right."
Issue 273: Sept 16th 2000

Pop star Shania Twain has an unusual beauty routine – she uses a moisturising cream designed for cows' udders. Bag Balm Udder Cream sets the singer back a mere £2.50 a jar. The news is unlikely to please cosmetics giant Elizabeth Arden, who pay Shania a fortune to promote their rather pricier products.
Issue 276: Oct 7th 2000

Mick Hucknall was forced to chop off his trademark dreadlocks after former Eastender's star Martine McCutcheon was sick all over them. The incident occurred when the Simply Red singer was giving a drunk McCutcheon a lift home from a concert. "I was sick everywhere, over and over again, but mainly over Mick and his famous red dreadlocks," admitted the actress. "I was later told he had to cut his dreads off because he couldn't get the smell out."
Issue 277: Oct 14th 2000

Mariah Carey has cemented her reputation as a demanding diva. At the MTV awards, the American singer not only insisted that she was greeted by a cheering crowd, but that kittens and puppies be provided for her to pet backstage. When asked to descend a staircase during the show, she snapped: "I don't do stairs."
Issue 278: Oct 21st 2000

Mel Gibson stunned movie bosses by denouncing his recent film, a thriller called The Million Dollar Hotel. The actor fumed that the film, which was co-written by U2's Bono, was "as boring as a dog's ass".
Issue 279: Oct 28th 2000

Actress Erica Leerhson took method acting a little too far for her role in Blair Witch II. When the film's director ordered his cast to write spooky anonymous letters to themselves, she did so with gusto. "I started writing myself letters, pretending to be a girl having an affair with my boyfriend," says the actress. Before long Leerhson had convinced herself of his infidelity. "I showed him one of the letters and confronted him. We had a row and I dropped him."
Issue 280: Nov 4th 2000

Sandra Bullock has become addicted to acupuncture, reports the Daily Star. The Hollywood actress spends £1,200 a week paying for two acupuncturists to follow her around the set of her new movie. "My obsession is very selfish," says Sandra, 35. "It's costing me all my savings, but while the money lasts I can't quit."
Issue 283: Nov 25th 2000

As Michael Douglas wed Catherine Zeta Jones last week, a former Page 3 girl stepped forward to tell The Sun about her "torrid" romps with the 56-year-old actor. Jenny Strachan, from Newcastle-upon-Tyne, who had a two-year affair with Douglas, said: "It was the best sex I ever experienced. I have been out with the comedian Jim Davidson and he was only Mr Average in bed. But Michael was something else. He is an amazing lover. Any woman lucky enough to share his bed would say he is the biggest and best they have ever experienced."
Issue 284: Dec 2nd 2000

Hollywood actors take each other pretty seriously, says the National Enquirer. Before doing an impersonation of Sean Connery in the film What Women Want, Mel Gibson contacted Sean to ask his permission. Sean said it would be fine – provided Mel donated $10,000 to one of his favourite charities. Mel told Paramount to send the cheque immediately.
Issue 289: Jan 13th 2001

Shannen Doherty is as volatile as ever, says the National Enquirer. When the former Beverley Hills 90210 star was arrested for drink-driving recently, she flew into such a rage she had to be 'hogtied', with her arms and legs behind her back. Shannen lashed out at officers, screaming: "Don't you touch me! I don't appreciate this treatment, and I will sue you! I can talk to any magazine in the world and any TV show and I can tell them just how horrible you people are!"
Issue 290: Jan 20th 2001

Hugh Grant, who plays the love interest in Bridget Jones's Diary, has a taste for plumper women. "I totally understand the Bridget attraction," he told The Sun. "I like a bit of meat with my gravy. To see a slightly grubby overweight girl in the office leaning over the photocopier with a little bit of coffee spilled down her skirt is very sexy."
Issue 302: April 14th 2001

Catherine Zeta Jones has had a face-lift at the age of 31, claims the Sunday People. The actress was snapped coming out of a plastic surgery clinic in Beverly Hills with a pink shawl hiding her swollen eyes. The Welsh star went under Dr Frank Kramer's knife to have her upper and lower eyelids lifted.
Issue 306: May 12th 2001

Charlie Sheen is back from the brink, says Playboy. At one point, the actor and son of Martin Sheen was addicted to drink, drugs and sex. He was consuming a pound and a half of cocaine every month and sleeping with hundreds of women – once bedding five at the same time. "I wouldn't recommend five at once," he says now. "There's just not enough guy to go round."
Issue 307: May 19th 2001

Jennifer Lopez's diva-ish behaviour has astounded the crew of her latest film, Enough, claims the National Enquirer. Lopez, 30, never goes anywhere without her assistant, a hairdresser, a make-up artist and a legion of bodyguards, who refer to her as "No 1". Cast and crew are under strict instructions not to look at or speak to her directly, says an insider, but her bodyguards "report every step she takes by walkie-talkie. 'No 1 has arrived at make-up'. 'No 1 has ordered a sesame bagel with light cream cheese.'"
Issue 310: June 9th 2001

Madonna initiated JFK Jr into the ways of kinky sex, claims a new book, Madonna: An Intimate Biography. On one occasion, says author J. Randy Taraborrelli, Madonna sneaked into JKK Jr's apartment, wrapped herself in clingfilm and lay on his sofa. When he came home, she purred: "Dinner's ready, John-John."
Issue 312: June 23rd 2001

Actress Mira Sorvino got into a vicious brawl with singer Maria Carey on the set of their new movie, Wise Girls. "Mariah was consistently late for work – and it drove Mira crazy," says a source. When Mariah turned up three hours late one day, Mira exploded, screaming: "I'm tired of your shit. You have no respect for your co-workers." Mariah hurled a salt shaker at Mira's head in response. "The next thing you know, the girls were rolling around on the floor, punching, scratching, pulling hair. It was a real cat fight."
Issue 316: July 21st 2001

Actress Sean Young underestimated the market when she posted an offer on her website for autographed used knickers at $19.99 a pop. Instead of the few hundred responses she'd expected, the star received a massive 3,500 orders. To meet the demand, she dutifully bought up entire lingerie counters and then spent several days slipping panties on and off, laundering them and signing them.
Issue 320: August 18th 2001

Drew Barrymore is so devoted to her dog, Flossie, that she is leaving it her $3m Beverly Hills home. The actress has felt indebted to Flossie ever since the dog saved her life by raising the alarm when her house caught fire in February. "Drew and her husband Tom love that dog more than anything in the world," says a friend. "They want to know she'll always have a roof over her head."
Issue 321: August 25th 2001

Lisa Marie Presley is refusing to marry Nicolas Cage without the consent of her father, Elvis Presley. The couple have been to 14 mediums in an attempt to win the King's blessing from beyond the grave. So far, Lisa Marie has failed to get in touch with Presley, and Cage is losing patience. "She's obsessed," he told a friend. "I've told her I can't take much more."
Issue 323: Sept 8th 2001

Gene Pitney is to record a song for Charlie Dimmock called Planting Love. Pitney, 60, whose hits include 24 Hours From Tulsa, fell for the blonde gardener after watching her on television. He told Capital Gold radio: "I watch her jiggle all the time on BBC America."
Issue 326: Sept 29th 2001

Even Jordan has her limits – and Hugh Hefner found them, says The Mirror. On her recent trip to LA, the British glamour model hit the town with Hef and his seven girlfriends. While they were cruising in his limo, the Playboy founder suggested that Jordan might like to)entertain him, but she flatly refused. "You have to draw the line somewhere," said an insider, "Jordan was sickened at the idea of writhing around in the car with a wrinkly old man and seven other girls. She knew then it was time to go home."
Issue 329: Oct 20th 2001

Lara Flynn Boyle doesn't appreciate constructive criticism, says the National Enquirer. The actress was recently stopped by a frumpy-looking fan in a Beverly Hills car park. While Flynn Boyle was signing her autograph, the fan said: "You're very pretty, but you don't eat enough!" She then pulled a hamburger out of her bag and handed it to her. Lara said: "I have something for you too", and handed the lady a little make-up case from her bag. Oblivious to the insult, the fan walked off, delighted with her gift.
Issue 331: Nov 3rd 2001

Sophie Ellis-Bextor was horrified when she spotted some of her old modelling photos hanging in the Stuart Phillips hairdressing salon in Covent Garden. The pictures were taken before she hit the big time, in exchange for a free haircut, and the pop star said she didn't "feel good" about them still being on display. The hairdresser refused to remove them, so she stormed in and took them down herself. A customer says: "I couldn't believe it when I saw Sophie armed with a screwdriver. She went around and angrily unscrewed the lot."
Issue 338: Dec 22nd 2001

George Clooney has developed a passion for lap-dancing clubs, claims the National Enquirer. The film star has reportedly become a regular guest at a Los Angeles strip joint called 4 Play, where he pays $130 for a "hot bed dance" in a private boudoir. "George really loves it here," says dancer Ivy. "He always has the hot bed dances. They're definitely worth the $130 because you get the girl for a minimum of five dances and it's private."
Issue 339: Jan 5th 2002

Julie Andrews' relations certainly know how to hit her where it hurts. Kayti Edwards – granddaughter of Andrews' husband Blake Edwards – decided to capitalise on the connection by posing for Hustler magazine dressed as Mary Poppins. Andrews is said to be furious, but Kayti is unrepentant. "If Julie and my grandfather had paid off my student loan, I wouldn't have done it," she told the magazine. "I am sure that Julie will always love me. If she can't, then that's pretty shallow."
Issue 343: Feb 2nd 2002

Pregnant glamour model Jordan has announced that she will give birth live on a pay-per-view internet site. The Page 3 girl is set to make millions from the event, which will earn her a place in history as the first British woman to deliver a baby live on screen. Anyone who misses the main event – scheduled for 16 May – will be able to buy a video of "edited highlights". Jordan says: "I want fans to share my joy."
Issue 344: Feb 9th

Naomi Campbell has smuggled drugs in and out of Britain, claims the News of the World. The supermodel's former assistant, Rebecca White, says Naomi routinely carried cocaine through airports and once asked White to carry some ecstasy for her. "She thought I would be untouchable because I was part of her entourage. She always got special treatment at airports and was whisked through without any fuss."
Issue 346: Feb 23rd 2002

Elizabeth Taylor is used to getting what she wants, says the National Enquirer. The Hollywood icon was out walking her Maltese dog, Sugar, recently when another Maltese came running up. The two dogs got along so well that Taylor immediately offered the owner $10,000 for her pooch. The woman refused, but agreed to bring her dog over twice a week for playtime.
Issue 351: March 30th 2002

Serbian pop star Goca Trzan burst into tears when, expecting a sellout crowd, she walked on stage at a Belgrade concert – and discovered only one man in the audience. The 30-year-old businessman had bought 4,000 tickets so that he could have a private concert. After recovering from the shock, Trzan gamely treated her fan to a full performance.
Issue 359: May 25th 2002

Kylie Minogue is starting to find the adulation of her bottom rather oppressive. "I don't understand what all the fuss is about," the Aussie singer told the Sunday People. "As far as I'm concerned, it does what it's meant to do, and it's in fairly good shape. But I often look in the mirror and think things aren't that great. I have got a bit of cellulite. It's only faint but I can see it if I look carefully."
Issue 361: June 8th 2002

Drea de Matteo who plays Adriana in The Sopranos, loves her dog, Cyrus, so much that she wouldn't let her vet castrate him, insisting on performing the operation herself. "I wasn't going to let a stranger touch him in that private spot with a knife," she says. She has kept the testicles preserved in a jar "in plain view so Cyrus knows they are there and not far away". After he dies, she plans to have the dog stuffed and mounted, with his testicles reattached.
Issue 363: June 22nd 2002

Ewan McGregor can't be bothered with gyms, says The Sun. Instead, the Star Wars actor does his keep-fit with wife Eve Mavrakis. "I keep in shape by shagging," he told the paper. "It's better than working out."
Issue 370: August 10th 2002

Jim Carrey is mourning the death of his hamster, says the Daily Star. The actor held a midnight funeral for the rodent on a beach in Malibu, sending his deceased pet Merle out to sea in a tiny burning boat – equipped with blankets and chocolate – to the strains of The Doors' song The End.
Issue 373: August 31st 2002

Courtney Love is guilt-stricken over the death of her dog, says the News of the World. The grunge rocker was horrified to learn that her adored pooch had perished after devouring one of her breast implants. Love had taken the implants home as a souvenir after having them removed – but the dog mistook them for a snack, with fatal consequences.
Issue 380: Oct 19th 2002

Victoria Beckham is basking in the gratitude of Britain's mothers, says The Sun. "I raised the awareness of designer wear among the younger generation," says Posh. "Mums come up to me and say, 'Thanks to you we are saving up for a Gucci dress for our daughter.'"
Issue 381: Oct 26th 2002

Tom Jones is fed up with women throwing their underwear at him, says the Daily Star. "When it began in the Sixties, it was authentic," says the Welsh crooner, who is always bombarded on stage by knickers thrown by female fans. "Nowadays they bring along a plastic bag with their underwear in it. It has nothing to do with enthusiasm any more. I actually take it as an insult."
Issue 382: Nov 2nd 2002

Tara Palmer-Tompkinson takes her inspiration from the foul-mouthed screen icon Mae West, says the Daily Star Sunday. Recently, she had a chance to use one of West's favourite putdowns when a weedy-looking man approached her in a nightclub and said: "I want to f**k you." Gazing down at him, Tompkinson coolly replied: "If you do and I ever find out about it, I'll be very angry."
Issue 384: Nov 16th 2002

Ben Affleck's devotion to Jennifer Lopez knows no bounds. The couple were shopping in LA last week when J-Lo nipped into a coffee shop for a pee. Minutes later she rang Affleck on his mobile complaining of "scratchy toilet paper". He was seen shortly afterwards crouching by the women's lavatory, pushing sheets of luxury loo-roll under the door.
Issue 392: Jan 18th 2003

Ryan Adams takes himself rather seriously, says Ananova.com. The ultra-cool British singer was performing in Nashville recently, when a member of the audience shouted out a request for Summer of '69 – the signature tune of Canadian rock star Bryan Adams. Furious, Ryan stopped the show and ordered the house lights to be turned on so that he could identify the culprit. He then paid the man $30 – the cost of his ticket – and ordered him to leave.
Issue 394: Feb 1st 2003

Celine Dion is launching her own perfume, reports the Daily Star. The company that makes the scent, Coty and March, describe it as a "romantic floral fragrance", but Dion sees it differently. "I wanted it to be feelings and memories," said the Canadian singer. "It smells like my mother's cooking, my husband, a warm fireplace and a new baby."
Issue 397: Feb 22nd 2003

Russell Crowe is doing his honeymoon on the cheap, says Ananova.com. Instead of flying off to an exotic destination, the Hollywood star is treating his new bride, Danielle Spencer, to a self-drive holiday around Australia. The newlyweds have been staying in a motel in Rockhampton town, where they were spotted at the Red Rooster restaurant drinking a £5 bottle of wine. "If I was a movie star, Rockhampton is the last place I'd come for a honeymoon," said a local.
Issue 405: April 19th 2003

Carly Simon is missing the limelight, says the National Enquirer. The singer was in a New York taxi recently when You're So Vain came on the radio. "That's me!" she told the driver. When he ignored her, she started singing along at the top of her lungs. But the cabbie wasn't impressed: he slammed on the brakes, pulled over and shouted, "Get out!"
Issue 406: April 26th 2003

Sharon Stone behaved like a true diva on a recent flight from London to LA, says Heat magazine. After summoning a stewardess by shouting, "Hey, girly! Girly!", the Hollywood star requested that the first class lavatory be reserved for her personal use and that her fellow passengers use the other toilets. Her request was refused.
Issue 407: May 3rd 2003

Demi Moore has been accused of sexually harassing an employee and then firing him when he spurned her advances, says the National Enquirer. Lawrence Bass, the former estate manager on Moore's Idaho ranch, has filed a complaint against the star, claiming: "Demi tried to seduce me – not once, but twice. And when I turned her down, she canned me."
Issue 410: May 24th 2003

Vinnie Jones really is a nasty piece of work, says The Mail on Sunday. The footballer turned actor was recently on a flight to Japan when a fellow passenger incurred his displeasure. Jones grabbed the hapless man by the neck and muttered: "I can have you killed for £500, mate." When a cabin crew member tried to intervene, Jones told her to back off, snarling: "Go and make some coffee like you're paid to."
Issue 412: June 7th 2003

Catherine Zeta-Jones's father is not best pleased that his son-in-law, Michael Douglas, has taken to calling him "Pops". "I think it's because he's two years younger than I am," says Douglas.
Issue 412: June 7th 2003

Kylie Minogue has a secret technique for keeping her famous bottom in shape, says the Daily Star. The pop princess visits a top London salon to have her buttocks "twitched" with hi-tech electrodes. The Ionithermie treatment begins with an oil massage, after which tiny electric pulses are applied to the muscles to make them relax and tense. To finish, Kylie has her bottom polished with a toning product.
Issue 415: June 28th 2003

Faye Dunaway is a hard taskmaster, says the Daily Mail. On the set of her new film, The Last Goodbye, the 62-year-old actress sent her assistant out to buy some plum tomatoes. When the girl returned with a box of plums by mistake, a furious Dunaway made her stand in the corner and then pelted her with the pieces of fruit, one by one.
Issue 419: July 26th 2003

Michael Jackson is tiring of his ivory tower, reports the Daily Star. In a recent attempt to be "normal" the singer hired an entire supermarket in California so he could "shop and be like everyone else and put things in a basket". He got his friends to pretend to be shoppers, and had his cousins dress up as bag packers. "It was fun," said the singer. "It gave me a chance to see what the real world was like, even though it wasn't the real world."
Issue 423: August 23rd 2003

Leah Wood, daughter of the Rolling Stone Ronnie, recently found herself obliged to offer her cleaning lady a bed for the night. While cleaning the kitchen, the woman tucked into a slice of leftover cake. Shortly afterwards, she came over all dizzy and had to lie down. Wood – realising she had unwittingly eaten her hash cake – insisted that she stay over until she was feeling better. "Leah was very apologetic in the morning," said a friend.
Issue 427: Sept 20th 2003

Sarah Jessica Parker has an unusual beauty secret, says Heat. The actress uses horse shampoo to keep her mane glossy. Her hairdresser, Anthony Dicky believes that Mane N'Tail shampoo (a snip at just $5 a bottle) is perfect for wiry, frizzy hair. "Tons of celebs are using it but they keep it under wraps, because they know it sounds so non-glam," says his assistant. Dicky recently started using another product on SJP's locks: Udder Butter, a deep-penetrating conditioner designed to prevent cow udders from chaffing.
Issue 437: Nov 29th 2003

Jordan – one of the contestants on I'm a Celebrity… Get Me Out of Here! – should be careful what she bares in the jungle, says the Daily Star. Doctors are concerned that, if leeches get to her 34FF bosoms, the silicone-enhanced model could explode. "She would need to be treated quickly if she was bitten on the chest," said one doctor. "I dread to think what would happen if her breasts swell."
Issue 445: Jan 31st 2004

Hugh Grant hopes to really sink his teeth into his next role, says the Daily Star. The actor is lined up to play cannibal Armin Meiwes, who was jailed last week for eating a man he met on the internet. Grant, 43, is keen to move away from romantic comedies. If he can secure the rights to Meiwes's story he will produce the film himself. He is, he says, in no doubt about who he would like to have on the menu. "Who wouldn't want to eat Brad Pitt?"
Issue 446: Feb 7th 2004

Tom Green must have a thing about Charlie's Angels, says the National Enquirer. The comedian – who used to be married to Drew Barrymore – is now stepping out with one of the original Angels: Farrah Fawcett. Green, 32, met the 57-year-old actress at a celebrity poker event, and the couple have been dating ever since. "They play cards, he makes her dinner," says a friend. "Stranger things have happened."
Issue 447: Feb 14th 2004

Kevin Costner's fiancée, Christine Baumgartner, is fed up with his penny-pinching, says the National Enquirer. Costner recently asked Giorgio Armani to whip her up a wedding dress for free, but Armani said he would only do it for $20,000. So the canny actor then tried his luck with Vera Wang. She offered to give him the dress for Jennifer Lopez's cancelled wedding, if he would pay $5,000 for alterations. Costner was baffled when Christine flew into a rage, said she would never marry in another woman's dress, and shouted: "You're just interested in getting a deal!"
Issue 450: March 6th 2004

Gina Gershon's attempts to build up an art collection aren't going well, says the Daily Mail. The actress recently spent £50,000 on two bullet-riddled phone directories by conceptual artist Tom Sachs. But no sooner had she put them on display than her cleaner threw them out and replaced them with two brand-new phone books. "There was nothing I could do but weep," says Gershon.

Issue 451: March 13th 2004

Jordan's "tell-all" memoirs could prove a disappointment, says the Daily Mirror. The glamour model – real name Katie Price – appeared at the London Book Fair this week to publicise her autobiography, Being Jordan. "The book is a chance to show the real me," she declared, posing with a pile of books. Unfortunately, the books then tumbled on the floor and fell open – revealing that all the pages were completely blank.

Issue 452: March 20th 2004

Naomi Campbell is one thrifty supermodel, says the National Enquirer. For her 34th birthday next month, Campbell is planning a big party in a private chateau in St Tropez. But she won't be picking up the tab herself: instead, she has written to potential sponsors, promising them "extensive media coverage and exposure" in return for their cash. For between $25,000 and $50,000, she says, the main sponsors will have "billing under [the] event title", plus up to ten tickets to the birthday party. Five thousand dollars gets your company's product into the guests' gift bags, plus two tickets to the party.

Issue 455: April 10th 2004

Daryl Hannah's finger dropped off at a recent Hollywood party, says the National Enquirer. The actress lost the tip of an index finger in a child-hood accident, and wears a prosthetic. It fell off during a party at the Bel-Air home of Disney boss Michael Eisner. Hannah hunted high and low before a fellow guest spotted the digit – on a table full of finger food.

Issue 464: June 6th 2004

Some people might not appreciate having wild child Courtney Love as a neighbour, says the National Enquirer. But rocker Lenny Kravtitz, who lives in the same Manhattan building as the 39 year-old singer, isn't complaining. "You open the elevator," he says, "and she's naked in there. It's great."

Issue 468: July 10th 2004

George Clooney's fans will go to any lengths to attract his attention, says the National Enquirer. The Hollywood heart-throb owns a villa on the shores of Lake Como, which is continually besieged by lusty Italian women, who throw themselves off boats and pretend to drown so that he will rescue them. The first time it happened, one of Clooney's staff dived in to save the floundering woman, but she shoved him away and got back on her boat in a huff. The star has now hired two full-time lifeguards to rescue the swooning fans.
Issue 470: July 24th 2004

Jack Nicholson loves his designer sunglasses, says the National Enquirer. So when a tiny screw fell out of his shades and into his salad while he was lunching in LA, the actor got straight on the phone to Gucci. "Just enjoy your lunch, Mr Nicholson," he was told: "I'll send someone." Moments later, a Gucci employee appeared at the restaurant, whipped out a miniature screwdriver and fixed the glasses. Nicholson gave him a $100 tip.
Issue 481: Oct 9th 2004

Joan Collins is harbouring a terrible secret: under her wig, she is completely bald. That, at least, is the story being put about by writer Molly Jong Fast, whose mother, Erica Jong, is one of Collins's oldest friends. Jong Fast says her exposure of Collins's secret is revenge: the actress teased her about her weight when she was a teenager.
"Joan should have known that obese 13-year-olds turn into menacing 24-year-olds with book contracts," she said.
Issue 489: Dec 4th 2004

Guy Ritchie has reportedly contacted Downing Street to ask for a meeting with Tony Blair. The film director apparently thinks Blair would benefit from Kabbalah, the mystical Jewish cult to which Ritchie and his wife Madonna belong. "Guy wants to tell the PM about the fantastic healing properties of Kabbalah Water, which could be useful in treating those injured in Iraq," a source told the Daily Mail. "Madonna says it even cured Guy's verrucas."
Issue 492: Dec 24th 2004

Celine Dion has discovered that she has a special gift for comforting the sick and dying, reports the National Enquirer. Some fans ring her up from their deathbeds; others have chosen to spend their final moments in her dressing room at Caesar's Palace in Las Vegas. "I heard their last breath," said the singer. "I feel very fortunate. I feel like I'm escorting them to heaven."
Issue 493: Jan 8th 2005

Kylie Minogue's gold hotpants have been insured for £1m. The shorts are the star attraction at an exhibition of Kylie memorabilia in Melbourne. They are being kept in a bulletproof display case, and there are guards on duty round the clock to protect them from pant pilferers.
Issue 495: Jan 22nd 2005

Pamela Anderson doesn't always see eye-to-eye with her friend Paris Hilton. "She's funny," Anderson told GQ magazine. "Last time I met her we were in a restaurant together. She slammed the menu down and screamed, 'I hate reading! Someone tell me what's on the menu!' I mean, I'm blonde but c'mon…"
Issue 512: May 21st 2005

Paris Hilton has ditched her canine companion of the past four years, Tinkerbell, for being too fat. The chihuahua has "ballooned" beyond its ideal weight of three and a half pounds, so the hotel heiress has sent it to live with her mother, and bought a dinkier one named Bambi. "Paris only likes them when they're very small," explained a source.
Issue 526: August 27th 2005

Mariah Carey has given her Jack Russell terrier his own chauffeur-driven Mercedes so that he can travel 3,000 miles from New York to Los Angeles in comfort. The diva had wanted Jack to fly First Class with her, but the airline refused to give him a seat. "They said, 'We'd only allow it for a famous dog,'" says Carey. "Please! He has three websites dedicated to him."
Issue 533: Oct 15th 2005

Cameron Diaz believes the British are a nation of wife-swappers. "Like, the British are really good at that," says the actress. "They are so incestuous. They pass around partners as if it was like popcorn at a movie. 'Do you want some?' It's just bizarre. But they are comfortable with it."
Issue 536: Nov 5th 2005

Katie Holmes is no longer welcome at the cinema, says the National Enquirer. The actress – who is pregnant by Tom Cruise – recently went to the movies with her Scientology 'minder', Jessica Rodriguez. After they sat down, an annoying hum filled the theatre. A manager stalked the aisles trying to track it down, then swung his torch on to Holmes. "Are you making that noise?" he hissed. Rodriguez explained that her friend was wearing a device that transmits soothing vibrations to the foetus, but the manager was unmoved. "I can't give you special treatment," he barked. You're annoying the customers." Refusing to pull the plug, the pair left the theatre.
Issue 538: Nov 19th 2005

Kate Beckinsale keeps her marriage alive by doing stripteases on the internet. When the British actress is filming away from her husband, director Len Wiseman, she puts on a private performance for him every night via web cameras. "It was Len's idea and he set them up," she told Playboy magazine. "He tells me what to wear each evening. There's no way we are keeping it clean. That's the whole point. It's like when you get a photocopier and you just have to do one of your bum. It's just one of those rules of life."
Issue 542: Dec 17th 2005

It seems Canadians are none too fond of Posh Spice. A novelty gift company in Canada has brought out a new range of lavatory paper featuring the faces of Osama bin Laden, Saddam Hussein – and Victoria Beckham. The Posh Wipes are luxuriously padded and bear the motto: "For posh poos."
Issue 544: Jan 7th 2006

Michael Jackson has been collaborating with the late Pope, reports The Mail on Sunday. The star has held secret meetings with the Catholic Church to discuss putting 24 prayers written by John Paul II to music. Jackson is said to have flown to Italy to sign a contract but fled when the press arrived. "We hoped the fact that we have been in contact with Michael Jackson would remain a secret," said Fr Giuseppe Moscati. "We are trying to sort it out."
Issue 550: Feb 18th 2005

Pearsall

This Sporting Life

Golfer Peter Belts His Ball Up a Sheep's Bum, said a headline in the
Daily Star. Peter Croke's ball driven from the tee at a Glamorgan Golf
Club, went 40 yards down the fairway "and straight up the sheep's
backside." The startled animal trotted off 416 yards to the 17th hole
helping Croke to win the hole and match.
Issue 3: June 10th 1995

Andre Agassi and Steffi Graf's relationship is on the rocks because of
his obsession with cleanliness, reports The National Enquirer. A friend
claims that when Agassi (above with Graf) does his laundry "he stirs
the soapy clothes with a broomstick and uses entire packages of
softener for a single load". The tennis star also fills ice cube trays with
imported spring water for fear of contaminating his drinks.
Issue 261: June 24th 2000

Britain's latest sporting hero is bricklayer Danny Teare. The 34-year-old
has claimed the world champion pea-throwing title after hurling a pea
a massive 29.10 metres at the championships in Lewes, Sussex.
"It's a dream come true," said Danny.
Issue 286: Dec 16th 2000

A wife-swapping club in Verona has been given a government Olympic
grant after styling itself as a sport and recreation association.
Issue 301: April 7th 2001

Racing driver David Coulthard is to give £3 million to the fiancée he lost after being caught having a bath with a busty blonde. According to friends, the Grand Prix star is so racked with guilt that he wants to make model Heidi Wichlinski financially secure for life.
Issue 305: May 5th 2001

Lucian Badalatu, a promising player with Romanian soccer team CSM Resita, has been named as the world's worst-paid footballer. While Real Madrid's Zinedine Zidane pockets £90,000 a week, 23-year-old Badalatu's contract lands him 4p a week – enough for a loaf of bread. He says that only the food parcels he gets from supporters prevent him from giving up.
Issue 317: July 28th 2001

Muhammad Ali has a trick for avoiding sexual temptation, says the National Enquirer. He takes a box of matches with him to parties. "I see a girl I want to flirt with, which is a sin, so I light my matches," he says. He then touches the flame with his fingers. "Just imagine that's going to be hell. Hell's hotter and it's for eternity."
Issue 340: Jan 12th 2002

Estonia has won the world wife-carrying championships for the fifth consecutive year. Meelis and Anna Tammre completed the 254-metre course, which included two hurdles and a chest-deep pool, in 64 seconds in front of a crowd of 6,000. The couple, who beat 35 others, used the trademark "Estonia carry" technique, in which the woman squeezes her thighs around the man's face while hanging down his back.
Issue 366: July 13th 2002

Ronaldo has revealed the secret of his incredible performances on the pitch, says The Sun: he limbers up in bed. The Brazilian footballer, who is married to the model Milene Dominguez, says: "Sex a couple of hours before the match is the key to success. The man has to be rather passive and just enjoy the experience. This relaxes him and makes him happy, which in turn gives him a whole load of energy."
Issue 378: Oct 5th 2002

In preparation for the 2008 Olympics, the Chinese government is cracking down on signs written in bad English. These include the KFC slogan "eat your fingers off" and a dentist's sign which boasts: "Teeth extracted by the latest methodists".
Issue 389: Dec 21st 2002

A Romanian football club is planning to control rowdy fans by installing a crocodile-filled moat around the pitch. Fourth division Steaua Nicolae Balcescu has been threatened with expulsion from the league after repeated pitch invasions. "This is not a joke," club chairman Alexandru Cringus warned fans. "We can get crocodiles easily enough and feed them on meat from the local abattoir."
Issue 391: Jan 11th 2003

Maria Sharapova makes the biggest racket on the tennis court, says The Sun. The 16-year-old Russian is the noisiest grunter in tennis, reaching a volume of 100 decibels – equivalent to the noise of an aeroplane landing. Sharapova was given a warning at Wimbledon after complaints by opponents, but she says she can't help herself: "I don't even know I'm doing it."
Issue 416: July 5th 2003

A prison football team in Thailand fought their way to a 5-5 draw against a team of soccer-playing elephants. The prisoners weaved through a forest of elephant legs to score the first goal. But the elephants manoeuvred the oversized ball easily, to level the game at 5 goals all. "The elephants are not the best players because they are quite slow," said trainer Pattarapon Meepan. "We train them every day to kick the ball and to keep from treading on other players."
Issue 478: Sept 18th 2004

A football match had to be abandoned after the referee sent himself off. Andy Wain gave himself a red card for squaring up to goalkeeper Richard McGaffin during a Sunday league game between Peterborough North End and Royal Mail AYL. "It was totally unprofessional," said Wain, 39. "If a player did that I would send him off, so I had to go."
Issue 497: Feb 5th 2005

A pessimistic Welsh rugby fan chopped off his testicles after his team beat England this week. Geoff Huish, 26, was so sure England would triumph that he told friends, "If Wales win, I'll cut my balls off." After the match he duly went home and severed his testicles with a knife before popping them in a bag and taking them back to his social club in Caerphilly. He is now recovering in hospital.
Issue 498: Feb 12th 2005

A football coach in Oregon, USA, is under investigation for licking the bleeding wounds of his student athletes. The teacher was suspended last year after licking a pupil's bleeding knee, but a full investigation was launched when a parent complained of "a pattern of wilful, repeated inappropriate behaviour".
Issue 503: March 19th 2005

An Australian woman claims that a kiss from a member of Uruguay's national soccer team left her blind. Louise Kelsey, 58, a hotel maid in Victoria, says that after the player grabbed and kissed her, she developed post-traumatic stress disorder, which aggravated a pre-existing eye condition. Kelsey has sued the hotel, where the incident allegedly occurred. Dr Robert Nave, testifying for the defence, told the court that if her story is true, "I would be happy to nominate this kiss to the Guinness Book of Records as the most powerful kiss in history".
Issue 529: Sept 17th 2005

Golfer Martin Franklin scored a hole in one at Clacton in Essex – with a little help from a crow. When his ball landed five feet from the hole, the bird picked it up and dropped it in. "I need all the help I can get," said Martin, "but this is going too far."
Issue 283: Nov 25th 2000

It Must Be Love

Firemen were called out for help by a woman who had handcuffed her lover to a bed in a sex romp. They took ten minutes to cut through the solid steel cuffs of the man scantily clad in boxer shorts. He turned out to be the firestation's accident adviser.
Issue 7: July 8th 1995

Wives in Malaysia are being urged to beat up their drunken husbands. Pathi Parvathi of Women Against Alcohol said: "We must love and serve them, but if it is necessary to break their hands or legs to make them give up liquor, we must do so." Perhaps the threat works – her husband is now sober.
Issue 17: 16th Sept 1995

A bride of six months, Ny Chong, has won a divorce after telling a court in Hegang, China: "My mother-in-law insisted on sleeping under our bed making sex impossible."
Issue 28: Dec 2nd 1995

A bored housewife in Perth, Australia placed an advertisement for sex in a lonely hearts magazine. She received just one reply – and a naked photograph – from her own husband.
Issue 36: Feb 3rd 1996

Mary Stewart got out of bed after giving birth and clobbered her husband with a saucepan, putting him in hospital. She told police in Sydney, Australia: "It was to pay him back for all the pain he made me go through having his baby."
Issue 42: March 16th 1996

Couples who want to make love in the hay can now buy an American spray that makes sheets smell of a barn.
Issue 105: June 7th 1997

Janet Thompson got so fed up of men walking out on her that she married herself at a ceremony in Los Angeles.
Issue 106: June 14th 1997

After being banned from smoking at home by his wife Sybil, Californian multi-millionaire Robert Brett has left his fortune to her providing she smokes four cigars a day for the rest of her life.
Issue 121: Sept 21st 1997

When a jealous killer escaped from a Barcelona jail, saying he was going to murder his wife's lover, 13 men demanded protection at the local police station.
Issue 126: Nov 1st 1997

When Mary Mitas's prison visits to her boyfriend were cut short, she showed she was sticking by her man – by superglueing herself to him. Mitas, 19, covered her hand with a tube of glue and grabbed her fiancée Ben Myers at Winchester jail. The couple had to be carted off to hospital to be separated.
Issue 127: Nov 8th 1997

After a four-month Internet romance, computer analyst Bill Perrar arranged to meet his cyber-sweetheart in Sydney, Australia. She turned out to be the woman he divorced eight years ago.
Issue 140: Feb 14th 1998

Pampered Italian teenager Luciano Pozuoli, 18, burned down his parents' £350,000 house in Sora, Italy, after his father bought him a Fiat for his birthday instead of a Mercedes.
Issue 150: April 25th 1998

When Chad Bibbings, 51, of Nebraska decided to record his cheating wife having sex and send the tape to their friends, he hid beneath her bed – but sustained concussion when the bottom of the bed kept slamming into him.
Issue 158: June 20th 1998

Andre Gurnam put an advert in a paper in Lyons, France, saying: "Ladies – write in if you are bored with the man in your life." Among the replies were letters from his wife and mistress.
Issue 161: July 11th 1998

The marriage of professional garden gnomes Angela and Austin Byrne is on the rocks because Angela refuses to sing their Fiddly Diddly song at children's parties for £20 an hour. "I've been singing it for four years and I'm sick of it," said the 4ft 6in Angela from her giant toadstool. "I feel there has to be a more sensible way to earn a living."
Issue 162: July 18th 1998

Karen Jones fell for Paul Matthews after spotting him in an M5 traffic jam. Karen, 24, held up her phone number and Paul, 25, did the same. They've now married in Wordsley, Staffs.
Issue 164: August 1st 1998

Environmentalist Dee Brophy is so fed up with men that she's decided to marry a tree. Six months ago she pronounced herself "engaged" to a strapping silver birch near her home in Streatham, South London. She is now searching for a vicar willing to carry out the ceremony. "As soon as I clapped eyes on it I knew this was the one for me," she said.
Issue 166: August 15th 1998

A bride-to-be cancelled her wedding on the Greek island of Crete after she caught her fiancé wearing her dress whilst engaged in a passionate embrace with the best man.
Issue 167: August 22nd 1998

Hendrick Bengtsson, who is deaf, tried to sever his wife's fingers because she nagged in sign language. Bengtsson, 53, now in jail in Stockholm, said: "I'd had enough. I would close my eyes but the moment I opened them she would start again."
Issue 173: Oct 3rd 1998

Liz Froh, 35, of Hamburg, Germany, couldn't understand why strange men kept calling up asking her out on dates. Her husband Ernst eventually confessed he had placed a lonely hearts ad in a magazine because he was leaving her and didn't want her to be lonely at Christmas.
Issue 178: Nov 7th 1998

Jonathan Whitlam, of Lowestoft, has given up dating girls to pursue his one true love – tractor spotting. Jonathan, 26, spends his days scouring the country for rare makes. Now, after covering 40,000 miles in five years, he has produced a gripping £15 tractor video. "Tractors are my first passion. They are more beautiful than any girl."
Issue 182: Nov 28th 1998

Dwight Domberly, a 65-year-old from Philadelphia, is suing his wife Judith for £40,000 for destroying his stash of Viagra. Judith, 64, claims she had "every right" to flush 300 of the £7 pills down the loo. She said: "Dwight lost interest in huffing and puffing six years ago. I enjoyed sleeping through the night without being woken up and hounded for sex. Then Dwight discovered Viagra and my life became hell."
Issue 187: Jan 16th 1999

Bride Sharon Lynch, 32, was so impressed by the music at her wedding reception that she ran off with the disc jockey. After dancing with DJ Paul Bonser at the pub reception in Newark, Notts, the mother-of-two went on honeymoon with him instead of her new husband Jim.
Issue 190: Feb 6th 1999

Bill and Tanya MacCauley went for counselling in Pretoria, South Africa, to patch up their marriage. But things didn't work out as planned. Halfway through a session, Dr Cedric Wayne became so infuriated by Mrs MacCauley's carping that he leapt out of his chair to help her husband beat her up. "She's the most annoying woman I have ever been around," Dr Wayne told arresting officers, after Mrs MacCauley was admitted to hospital with concussion, a broken collarbone and three fractured ribs.
Issue 192: Feb 20th 1998

An Italian wife faces jail for refusing to make love to her husband. Pina Corlanda, 37, is being sued by her husband of 17 years, Salvatore ,44, under a little used law making it illegal for wives to ban lovemaking. "She's been saying no for eight months, she's a criminal," he told a court in Cassino.
Issue 207: June 5th 1999

One-legged lover Pierre Mercier, 51, died after hopping for a mile through Paris to escape a furious husband who found him in bed with his wife.
Issue 209: June 19th 1999

Trucker Heiner Beck is seeking a divorce after he drove into Berlin's red-light district looking for a prostitute – and found his wife.
Issue 211: July 3rd 1999

Angler Piet Huens was found guilty of spanking his wife with a live eel in Gothenburg, Sweden, and fined £100 for cruelty to the eel.
Issue 219: August 28th 1999

A couple of 87-year-olds in Chicago were granted a divorce after 66 years when they told the judge: "We waited till the kids were dead."
Issue 230: Nov 13th 1999

Frederico Piacci, 26, was granted a divorce in Milan, Italy, because his wife demanded two days' notice before making love and then gave him a ten-minute limit, using an egg timer.
Issue 234: Dec 11th 1999

Van driver Heiner Zimmerman picked up a prostitute and found it was his wife Karin. She told a divorce court in Frankfurt, Germany: "Now I know what he gets up to."
Issue 243: Feb 19th 2000

A couple won themselves a divorce in a radio competition after proving that they wanted it more than any other entrants. Kath Rose, of Sale in Greater Manchester, complained that husband Darren Wilson always left the lavatory seat up and hogged the TV remote control, while Wilson complained about the sound of his wife's breathing. Key 103 radio will now meet the cost of their divorce.
Issue 244: Feb 26th 2000

Beverly Dodds married Keith Redman after his 8,500th proposal. During their 24 years together, 43-year-old Keith left romantic notes around the house, popped the question during candlelit dinners, and sometimes asked while the couple were watching TV. Beverly said: "I was frightened of committing myself."
Issue 246: March 11th 2000

Professional body builder Johan Andersson of Stockholm is suing his girlfriend for secretly feeding him the female hormone oestrogen after a big row. "The next thing I knew I had baby-soft skin and a bustline," says Andersson. But his girlfriend is unrepentant. "I don't know why he's so upset. We were getting along much better. We were going to take cookery classes together."
Issue 250: April 8th 2000

Anne Jonsson, 21, gave husband Lars 23, a broken nose after he refused to go to a rally against domestic violence in Stockholm, Sweden.
Issue 253: April 29th 2000

Alijar Hajatz lost his wife in a bet over a football game. Hajatz, from Tirana, Albania, was so convinced of the outcome of an Argentina vs Bulgaria match that he staked his 24-year-old wife Marsha on it. "I was a bit short of cash," he explained. When Bulgaria thrashed Argentina 3-2, his rival, an Iranian businessman, claimed his prize. Marsha knew nothing of the bet until she was whisked away in a car. "There really wasn't much I could do about it. I'll miss her but I've got to get on with my life," said Hajatz.
Issue 254: May 6th 2000

A 32-year-old Californian has been arrested for impersonating his wife. When his estranged spouse took out a restraining order against him, Joshua Marete Mutama was so upset that he went to court dressed as his wife, complete with long, black wig, and, adopting a high falsetto voice, tried to dupe the clerk of the court into revoking the order.
Issue 255: May 13th 2000

Sandra Norman, 39, from Christchurch, Dorset, was deluged with replies from dodgy men when her lonely heart ad for a "caring gentleman" appeared as "caning gentleman".
Issue 260: June 17th 2000

A youth who threatened to jump off Hammersmith Bridge after splitting up with his girlfriend was persuaded down after an hour when police offered him a pair of new trainers. As he perched on a ledge above the Thames, he tried the Reeboks on for size and decided life was not so bad after all.
Issue 262: July 1st 2000

A divorce judge in Memphis, Tennessee, has ruled that a husband owns his wife's clothes and can strip her in public if she leaves him.
Issue 264: July 15th 2000

Mary Shepherd never let her late husband Peter smoke in their home in Los Angeles. In his will Peter has now left her £6 million, but only on condition that she smokes six cigarettes a day for the whole of next year.
Issue 269: August 19th 2000

Berliner Heidi Berger is divorcing her husband for being unable to satisfy her sexual needs. "Hans is a good man – but worn out," says Heidi, 100. "We've been married 69 years but the last five have been very frustrating." Her husband has taken the news well. "Thank God it's over," says Hans, 101. "That woman is an animal."
Issue 270: August 26th 2000

After three operations have failed to stop him snoring, Graham Warann is taking drastic action. He is building an extension to his house in Totton, Hampshire, so that his wife can get some sleep. "There were a few sniggers when I applied for planning permission," he says, "but they understood."
Issue 276: Oct 7th 2000

A student doctor in Romania is hiring himself out to girls who cannot find a suitable boy to take home to their parents. For 500,000 lei (£12) plus expenses, Victor Paiu will go home with a girl and pretend to be her boyfriend. His customers must sign a contract promising they will not try to sleep with him.
Issue 281: Nov 11th 2000

Elizabeth Froh, 34, received calls from dozens of men asking her out on dates after her husband Ernest placed a lonely hearts ad in the local paper. Ernest, from Vienna, Austria, had decided to leave her and didn't want her to be alone at Christmas.
Issue 285: Dec 9th 2000

Twice-divorced Mitch Hallen claims to have finally found true love after marrying his television set. Mitch, 42, promised to "love, honour and protect" his set in a ceremony witnessed by a dozen friends and performed by a priest at his home in Melbourne, Australia.
Issue 285: Dec 9th 2000

Newlywed Neil Hutchinson had his testicle bitten off in a brawl with a woman at a party, but he was so drunk he didn't notice. A police-man called to stop the fight in Newcastle said: "You won't believe what I've just found on the carpet. If that's what I think it is, he's in trouble."
Issue 286: Dec 16th 2000

New Yorker Alvin Eykers is divorcing his wife Judith because her psychic powers put too much strain on their marriage. "She'd finish my sentences before I got the words halfway out of my mouth," says Eykers. "I could never surprise her with a gift for Christmas or her birthday and I could never get away with even the littlest white lie. It was like she had a peephole into my mind." The crisis came when Judith accused him of having an affair with his firm's receptionist. Eykers insists: "I haven't touched her or even said two words to her – yet."
Issue 292: Feb 3rd 2001

An Ohio woman, Addie Crawley, got a shock when her ex-husband – who had been missing for 20 years – suddenly appeared from his cubbyhole hiding place in their former marital home. Thinking 48-year-old Ben Holmes was a ghost, Crawley drew her .22 handgun and shot him. He survived, later explaining in court that he had lived in the same house as his ex for several years, but hid himself whenever she was around. He had emerged to claim his share of the property.
Issue 299: March 24th 2001

Her face was so covered with soot that Melbourne fireman Jeff Urbank didn't realise the woman he had rescued from a burning house was his ex-wife. "When I recognised her voice I was stunned," said Jeff. "I had forgotten how beautiful she was." The couple have since remarried.
Issue 302: April 14th 2001

Sickly German folk singer Christian Anders is renting out his nubile girlfriend in order to fund a liver transplant. The 56-year-old singer has struck a deal with millionaire Michael Leicher, who will have free access to 20-year-old Jenna Kartes's bed for the next year in return for the £150,000 operation fee. Kartes is surprisingly sanguine about the deal. "I will sleep with Michael because I love Christian," she says. "Why should I feel like a prostitute about it?"
Issue 312: June 23rd 2001

Romanian housewife Fevronia Stoleru, 18, burned her drunk husband Mircea's shoulder with an iron when he fell asleep without making love. Mircea, 48, needed hospital treatment but is not pressing charges. "It serves me right," he said.
Issue 317: July 28th 2001

A divorcée in Port Talbot held a rooftop protest to draw attention to philandering in the town. Stephen Gammond, who claims that single men in the area prey on married women while their husbands are at work, strapped himself to his chimney for five hours, with a banner reading: "Down with Jack the Lads!" He took to the roof after losing his second wife to a neighbour. "The town is full of philanderers," he said. "It's a wife-stealing community."
Issue 323: Sept 8th 2001

A court in Swaziland has ordered a man to improve his performance in bed to satisfy both his wives. The case followed a furious row between Alfred Madolo's wives over who was getting the most conjugal action. President of the court Prince Jahamnayama ruled that Madolo only had himself to blame, having "dangled his penis" before the women of Swaziland, and said that he now had a duty to meet the "challenge" of polygamy.
Issue 331: Nov 3rd 2001

Sandi Canesco, a 26-year-old widow from Sydney, has had the ashes of her husband, Dustin, sewn into her breast implants so that she can keep him close to her heart.
Issue 332: Nov 10th 2001

A shopping centre in Renfrew, Scotland, is providing surrogate boyfriends to escort women round the shops. "The Shopping Boyfriend is the ultimate retail therapist: enthusiastic, attentive and admiring," says a spokeswoman. "He will browse with the girlfriend for hours on end." Real boyfriends can be dropped off at a "boyfriend creche", where they can play video games and read lads' magazines.
Issue 334: Nov 24th 2001

A bridegroom died during his wedding ceremony in Iran as he licked honey from his bride's finger, a custom to ensure that life together starts sweetly. He choked on her false fingernail.
Issue 338: Dec 22nd 2001

When Anthony McKenzie from Cheshire discovered a text message saying "I love you" on his wife's phone he exploded into a jealous rage. He accused her of having an affair and head-butted her, before remembering that he had sent the message himself. Mrs McKenzie is filing for divorce.
Issue 341: Jan 19th 2002

A woman from Colorado has filed for divorce after discovering her husband had faked being deaf and dumb for two years. Bill Drimland admitted in court that he had carried out the subterfuge in order to escape "constant nagging from his wife".
Issue 349: March 16th 2002

Laren Sims from Florida has launched a lawsuit from the grave. She hanged herself while awaiting trial for the murder of her husband. But she left a note instructing her lawyer to sue the jail for failing to prevent her suicide.
Issue 354: April 20th 2002

A Romanian man has divorced his wife of 30 years because she forgot to cook him a roast lamb for Easter dinner. Florian Paun, 59, launched proceedings because wife Marioara failed to prepare his favourite dish. "Imagine how I felt when I saw that all my friends had delicious roast lamb on their tables at Easter and I did not," he said. "She ruined my holiday and I cannot continue to live with her."
Issue 361: June 8th 2002

A New York widow has found a novel way to deter carjackers: she buckles her late husband's corpse into the passenger seat beside her. "Leonard always liked the open road," says Gloria Trenchley, "so keeping him in the car just seemed like the most natural thing in the world. I was told that, as long as I avoid long road trips in the middle of summer, Lenny should last the way he is for many years."
Issue 363: June 22nd 2002

A pair of Siamese twins have found love with the same man. Cape Town's Karen and Nikki Stafford have both settled down with trucker Ron Bullock. "Nikki loves Ron's romantic side," said Karen. "And he makes me lAugusth." Ron is equally complimentary. "Being with both Nikki and Karen is like love in stereo."
Issue 364: June 29th 2002

Trevor Tasker's steamy online romance took a turn for the worse when he flew to the US to marry his cyber girlfriend. Instead of the 30-year-old beauty he was expecting, Tasker, 27, was greeted at the airport by 65-year-old Wynema Shumate, who weighs 20 stone. Worse, when she took him back to her flat, he discovered that she kept the dead body of her former flatmate in her freezer. Shumate has been jailed, and Tasker has vowed never to go online again.
Issue 374: Sept 7th 2002

A Belgian man who fell in love with his primary school teacher when he was a boy has finally won her affections. Minne Herv, 42, fell for Daniella Waltens when he was six and she was his 18-year-old teacher. Thirty-six years later, the couple are engaged to be married. "When I saw her again after all that time I got the same goose bumps as I did when I was six," says Herv. "I always knew that I would end up marrying Miss Waltens."
Issue 379: Oct 12th 2002

An American psychoanalyst is setting up a dating service in which singles will be matched by their therapists. Clients of TheraDate will be assessed on factors such as obsessiveness, defence mechanisms and nervous tics. The founder, Frederick Levenson, believes that the idea is a sure-fire winner. "The smartest people are the ones in therapy," he says. "They're wonderful people, very bright, very funny."
Issue 376: Sept 21st 2002

A Sri Lankan widower has taken over all his late wife's duties – including breast-feeding their baby. Mr B. Wijeratne, 38, astonished villagers in Walapanee with his biological feat. "My child rejected the bottled milk I tried feeding her," he says. "I couldn't bear her crying so I offered her my breast. That's when I discovered that I could breastfeed her." Doctors believe his unique ability to produce milk may be due to a hyperactive prolactine hormone.
Issue 383: Nov 9th 2002

A Filipino man made the ultimate sacrifice to prove his fidelity to his wife – he cut off his penis. The man, from the village of Malasiqui, severed his penis, wrapped it in paper and delivered it to his in-laws' house, where his estranged wife is staying. He shouted: "So you will not suspect I am courting another girl" and ran off. Police are keeping the penis on ice until the man is found.
Issue 399: March 8th 2003

A Romanian man whose wife ran off with a Greek waiter has vowed to spend the rest of his life in a hole in the ground. Sandu Tudose, 74, has dug a hole in the garden of his farm in Mera, central Romania, and fitted it with a small lavatory, heater and tap. His shopping is delivered once a week and a neighbour takes away his rubbish.
Issue 405: April 19th 2003

A German man was cautioned by police after using a World War II air-raid siren to drown out his nagging wife. "She never let me get a word in edgeways, so in the end I cranked up the siren and let rip," said the 73-year-old, who had the 220-volt siren installed on his roof. "After that, she calmed down."
Issue 410: May 24th 2003

A Connecticut woman spent her wedding night behind bars after going on a drunken rampage at her reception. Adrienne Samen smashed her cake, spat on her ring, broke seven vases, and lay on her car shouting "I cannot believe I married you," before being arrested. The bride, who faces criminal charges, is now on honeymoon.
Issue 424: August 30th 2003

A newlywed who found her husband in bed with her mother has ventured down the aisle again – as a bridesmaid at their wedding. Alison Greenhowe, from Arbroath, was happily married for ten days until she found her husband George in bed with her 44-year-old mother Pat. "Everyone makes mistakes," she says. "I've lost a husband, but I've gained a father."
Issue 428: Sept 27th 2003

A Portuguese wife is facing jail after pretending to have been kidnapped in order to snatch a few hours with her lover. The 21-year-old woman, who hasn't been named, sneaked off to see her lover while at the cinema with her husband, telling him she was popping to a shop. She called home the next morning, saying she had been kidnapped by two Eastern European men, but had managed to escape and would be back soon. When she finally got home, she found the house full of police, who interrogated her until she confessed everything.
Issue 441: Dec 27th 2003

A Brazilian football referee is facing divorce proceedings after pulling out a pair of lacy knickers instead of a red card during a match. Carlos Jose Figueira Ferro was trying to send off a player during an amateur match in Anama. But he whipped a pair of red undies out of his pocket instead, and then fled the pitch in shame. Despite his insistence that he had never seen the knickers before, his wife, who was watching the match, has filed for divorce.

Issue 447: Feb 14th 2004

An Indian man is about to take his school exams for the 38th time, after vowing at the age of 20 that he would not marry until he had passed them. Shivdan Yadav, of Khohari village in Rajasthan, had a bride lined up when he first took the exams – but after three years her family lost interest and found a replacement groom.

Issue 452: March 20th 2004

An angry mother burst into a pub in Wales brandishing a pistol, because her son was late for Sunday lunch. Paula Williams, 37, waved the gun at drinkers at the Golden Lion in Nantyglo, Gwent, but 18-year-old Gareth had already left. "I don't think she'd have harmed me," he said later. "She has a short fuse but a heart of gold. And she does a good roast."

Issue 456: April 17th 2004

A pensioner was saved from an alligator attack by her fearless husband. Jane Keefer, 74, was working in her garden in Sanibel, Florida, when the ten-foot beast lunged at her and dragged her into a nearby lagoon. Her husband William, 78, dived into the water and wrestled the alligator's jaws open. The creature was later captured and destroyed.

Issue 458: May 1st 2004

An Indian man who has 90 wives wants ten more to "complete his century". Udaynath Dakshiniray, 80, of Orali in Orissa, says: "It's not to have my name in the record books but for a social mission. In a country where unmarrieds are looked down upon, I help them overcome social stigma and harassment."

Issue 460: May 15th 2004

A Chinese man sued his wife for £55,000 after discovering that she had had plastic surgery before they met. Jian Feng, 38, was "horrified" when his pretty wife gave birth to an ugly daughter. He accused her of having an affair, but she confessed to having had £70,000 worth of surgery in South Korea, and showed him a picture of how she used to look. He filed for divorce immediately, and then successfully sued her for deceit. The couple had married two years earlier, after a whirlwind romance.

Issue 463: June 5th 2004

It is a crime in Bangladesh for an unmarried couple to check into the same hotel room. So when Mominur Chowdhury was caught sneaking his girlfriend Shelley into a hotel room in Rajshahi, he was frog-marched down to the nearest cop shop and told to marry Shelley or face prosecution. He chose to propose, and the marriage ceremony then took place in the police station itself.
Issue 475: August 28th 2004

A couple from the US state of Maryland have "raised" a Cabbage Patch doll as their only son for 19 years. Pat and Joe Posey – who already have a grown-up daughter – treat Kevin the doll just like a human. He has his own playroom, a red mini Chevrolet Corvette car, a pet dog, a full wardrobe and a savings fund for when he goes to college. "With every kid that you adopt, you promise to love them and be a good parent," says Pat. "And that's what we did with Kevin."
Issue 476: Sept 4th 2004

A devout Hindu is carrying his mother on a 17-year pilgrimage to all of India's holy places. Kailashgiri Brahma-chari, who carries his blind mother in a basket, has travelled 3,750 miles since leaving his home town in Madhya Pradesh eight years ago, and expects to complete the journey in 2013. "He's a nice son, but I am getting tired," says his mother, 60. "Sometimes I feel like going back home."
Issue 477: Sept 11th 2004

A Romanian woman has upset her late husband's family by digging up his body and selling the grave. The woman, from Cristesti, reportedly dumped his remains outside the cemetery, saying she needed the money from the burial plot. His outraged family plans to rebury him elsewhere. "Did I do anything wrong? Was that a crime? I don't think so," the widow told a local newspaper. "I only dug him out because he was my husband – mine. I lived with him for 20 years, and not his family."
Issue 480: Oct 2nd 2004

A British couple has set a record for the shortest marriage – just 90 minutes. Victoria Anderson and Scott McKie began arguing as soon as they arrived at the reception in Stockport. The bride smashed the groom over the head with an ashtray and he then hurled a hat-stand at the bar "like a javelin". Staff called the police and the groom was arrested and charged with GBH after head-butting an officer. Meanwhile, the bride went home, cancelled the honeymoon in Corfu and filed for divorce.
Issue 490: Dec 11th 2004

On her deathbed, Geraldine Kelley decided to come clean with her children. Their father had not, as they thought, died in a car crash in 1990. "Where is he then?" they asked. "Well," said Mrs Kelley, "he's in a freezer at Planet Self Storage in Somerville, Massachusetts, and I killed him." Police have since recovered his remains.
Issue 489: Dec 4th 2004

A radio DJ's wife sold his £25,000 car on eBay for 50p, after she heard him flirting with Jodie Marsh on air. Kerrang! Radio's Tim Shaw jokingly told the glamour model that he would leave his wife and children for her. His furious wife, Hayley, immediately posted an advert for his Lotus Esprit Turbo on eBay, and sold it within minutes. "I didn't care about the money," she said. "I just wanted to get him back." A Kerrang! spokesman said the DJ was "absolutely gutted".
Issue 517: June 25th 2005

A man who tried to sit an exam for his sister was caught because his fake bosoms were too big. The unnamed man disguised himself as a girl to take the entrance exam for a journalism degree at Moscow State University. But Yasen Zasursky, head of the department, said the girl's "outstanding feminine features" and breasts of "incomparable proportions" aroused suspicion. The man and his sister have both been barred from the university for cheating.
Issue 519: July 9th 2005

Two lesbians who had a blazing row in public – by draping an assortment of banners over a motorway bridge – have announced that they are back together. The exchange started several weeks ago, when a banner reading: "Wendy, I want a divorce, JBS" appeared on a bridge over the A27 near Brighton. It was swiftly replaced by one reading: "No way. You are the cheat. Wendy." A third suggested: "I reckon we should meet." The last banner is addressed to those motorists who had been following the tiff, and reads: "Thanks for the support – we're back together, Wendy & Jenny."
Issue 535: Oct 29th 2005

A Munich judge threatened to convict a defendant after falling in love with his girlfriend. The 63-year-old judge, known only as Wolfgang W, took the 30-year-old woman out for dinner during her boyfriend's robbery trial, and then sent her a text saying: "I could lock him up for a long time, so that you can get some peace." He has been taken off the case and faces a fine for misuse of office.
Issue 549: Feb 11th 2006

Political Corrections

Transsexuals have won the right to carry both male and female travelcards on the London Underground. The decision follows complaints from transsexuals about difficulties with ticket inspectors. Meanwhile cross-dressers will be glad to learn that a summer school is offering lessons is designing dresses for men. It promises to teach transvestites the skills they need to make their own outfits.
Issue 1: May 27th 1995

A lollipop lady in Devon refused to help two 10 year-old boys cross the road because they were foreigners.
Issue 3: June 10th 1995

A Malaga-based dog-food firm cancelled its search for a (human) beauty queen when not a single entrant came forward. The company, which advertised the contest under the name "Bitch of 1996", remains baffled by the lack of interest.
Issue 68: Sept 14th 1996

In recognition of his right to religious tolerance, Devil worshipper Eldon Clearmore has been allowed by his boss in San Francisco to go to work wearing nothing but plastic horns, a fur tail and a cape.
Issue 123: October 11th 1997

A fruit seller was ordered to eat a hay bale after he made his horse ill feeding it junk food. A court at Campana, Argentina, heard the animal needed emergency surgery after being fed chips, pizza and dohnuts.
Issue 166: August 15th 1998

Romanian airline bosses have sacked 131 stewardesses because their bottoms had grown too big for their uniforms. Another 29 expanding stewardesses saved their jobs with an emergency diet of cabbage soup.
Issue 185: Jan 2nd 1999

A father who demanded compensation from a bus firm for ruining his son's school jacket received a reply full of expletives. The letter on East Yorkshire Motor Services headed paper read: "We find your claim to be utter bollocks... and believe your son to be lying. We also believe that you are trying to rip us off. So get f****d."
Issue 201: April 24th 1999

Road sweepers in Milan have been told to shorten their broom handles to stop them spending so much time leaning on them to chat.
Issue 202: May 1st 1999

Texan businessman Donald J. Templow has stretched the Second Amendment – the right to keep and bear arms – to its limits by amassing an arsenal of Russian nuclear warheads. The US government is powerless to act. "As we have never actually seen the weapons in his possession we have no proof he has violated statutes," said a spokesman. Templow says he has no plans to back down. "If Mexico invades, I'm not waiting for Washington to take action."
Issue 267: August 5th 2000

Slim, beautiful women and handsome men have been banned from the town pool in Siani, near Florence, because they embarrass fat and ugly swimmers. Manager Paulo Scio said: "It is very popular. Good-looking people can't come in and the rest feel happy."
Issue 268: August 12th 2000

A recent Qantas flight was nearly grounded by a confusion over names, reports the Sydney Morning Herald. Mr Gay, a Qantas employee, was taking advantage of the company's Free Flight programme when he found his seat occupied by a paying passenger. Unfazed, Mr Gay found another seat, unaware that all Free Flighters were being asked to get off due to overbooking. A stewardess approached the seat where Mr Gay was supposed to be, and asked the occupant, "Are you Gay?" The man shyly nodded that he was and was told to get off the plane. Mr Gay, overhearing the conversation, said: "You've got the wrong man. I'm Gay." This caused an angry third passenger to yell: "Hell, I'm gay too! They can't kick us all off." More passengers joined the fray, yelling that

Qantas had no right to remove gays from their flights. Qantas refused to comment on the incident.
Issue 268: August 12th 2000

A county council in Wales has produced a leaflet that explains the meaning of "daylight". Carmarthenshire council's road-safety brochure says that daylight is all times other than darkness. It also defines pedestrians as road users on foot.
Issue 297: March 10th 2001

Lars Black, gender equality adviser to the Swedish government, has denied harassing an air hostess during a flight from Stockholm to New York. But he admits being sick into the lap of the minister of agriculture, who was also on the flight.
Issue 298: March 17th 2001

The men of Macclesfield, North Carolina, have been ordered to grow beards by next week or face a $25 fine. Beard-growing on special occasions is an old English custom, say local councillors, who passed the law to celebrate the town's centenary.
Issue 302: April 14th 2001

Specially commissioned braille posters promoting equal treatment for the blind are on display at Truro Leisure Centre. Alas, full-sighted people cannot read the posters because they are written in braille, and neither can the blind because the limited-edition posters have been hung behind glass covers to protect them.
Issue 303: April 21st 2001

The charity People for the Ethical Treatment of Animals has won the right to use the web address peta.org from rival pressure group People Eating Tasty Animals.
Issue 323: Sept 8th 2001

The state of Florida has banned the sport of dwarf-tossing, but not everyone approves. Local little person Dave "the Dwarf" Flood, who stands at 3ft 2in, has issued a lawsuit to overturn the ban, saying it deprives him of his income. "This is a free country. If I want to earn money by allowing drunks to fling me through the air on to a mattress, then that's my business."
Issue 356: May 4th 2002

Lithuanian women were celebrating last week after the government finally scrapped a law which required women to undergo gynaecological examinations in order to gain a driving licence.
Issue 360: June 1st 2002

A Las Vegas ranch is charging men up to $10,000 to shoot naked women with paintballs, in a sport it calls Hunting for Bambi. The women – who get paid $2,500 per hunt if they don't get hit, and $1,000 if they do – run around the Nevada desert in nothing but goggles, to protect their eyes. "The main goal is to be as true to nature as possible," says the game's inventor, Michael Burdick. "I don't go deer hunting and see a deer with a football helmet on, so I don't want to see one on my girl either."
Issue 419: July 26th 2003

The Kiwi sport of "Leprechaun hurling" is under threat, after protests from the Little People of New Zealand. The pressure group claims the sport – in which little people volunteer to be covered in oil and propelled head-first down a 20ft-long slide – is degrading.
Issue 429: Oct 4th 2003

A grandfather with a silvery beard was barred from buying fireworks because he could not prove he was over 18. Anthony Marthlin, 58, who has arthritis and uses a wheelchair, showed his registered disabled card to staff at the Basingstoke Co-op, but was told it was no good because it did not have his date of birth.
Issue 432: Oct 25th 2003

White socks have been banned at the Dutch finance ministry because they offend "the limits of decent dress behaviour". But not everyone is happy with the new ruling. "I can think of nothing nicer than a bright, shiny pair of white socks to set off a black pair of shoes," said one civil servant.
Issue 444: Jan 24th 2004

Police officers in India are being offered a monthly bonus of 35p if they cultivate a moustache. Officers in Jhabua, Madhya Pradesh, are being encouraged to grow whiskers as a form of "non-verbal communication" with the public. "Facial hair adds to the overall authority of officers," explained superintendent Mayank Jain, adding that "the shape of the moustache will be monitored to prevent it from taking on a mean or vulgar twist."
Issue 445: Jan 31st 2004

German brothels have been told they must offer work experience and trainee posts if they want to continue doing business. A new government bill requires all companies with more than ten staff to provide on-the-job apprenticeships. Since prostitution is not officially recognised as a profession, the Ministry for Education, Training and Research wants brothels to offer internships in book-keeping, sales and marketing.
Issue 460: May 15th 2004

An Iowa doctor is refusing demands by women patients that he remove framed Playboy centrefolds from his waiting room. "I put those pictures up simply as examples of healthy female bodies," said general practitioner Dr Wilbur Quately. "It gives my patients something to aspire to." But his women patients say that if that's the case, he should also have photos of naked men. "Come on," said Quately, "that would be gay."
Issue 470: July 24th 2004

Actors in Vietnam have been banned by the government from having shaved heads, unkempt or dyed hair, and other "hairstyles which inflict horror".
Issue 472: August 7th 2004

Romanian police want to ban women over 60 from going topless on the beach, saying it is "ugly" and may deter tourists. Officers patrolling the Black Sea coast say they have had scores of complaints about pensioners stripping off in the sun. "It's always a pleasure to see a beautiful young woman topless on the beach," says officer Ionut Popescu. "But there are more old women going topless. I find it sometimes quite repulsive. I can understand the idea of wanting to get a uniform tan, but old women should simply give up on it."
Issue 473: August 14th 2004

The headmaster of a school in Alaska has been sacked for having himself beaten in the presence of two of his pupils. The boys in question had been hauled in front of Steve Unfreid, of the Matanuska Christian School, after being caught snogging their girlfriends in the locker room for the second time in a week. "I've let the atmosphere get too lax," said Unfreid, before taking off his belt, and instructing a fellow teacher to discipline him "like you would discipline your own son". Unfreid told the teacher to stop only when the boys acknowledged their mistake.
Issue 487: Nov 20th 2004

MPs in Hungary are considering introducing a ban on jokes about blondes following a series of demonstrations. "People are banned from discriminating against Jews and blacks," said a spokesman for the Blonde Women's Movement, which is leading the campaign. "Why not grant blondes the same protection?"
Issue 489: Dec 4th 2004

Kraft Foods has withdrawn a range of sweets shaped like animals that have been hit by cars. The US company was swamped by complaints from animal rights activists after the launch of "Road Kill Candy" – a fruity selection of squashed chickens, squirrels and snakes with tyre tracks across their corpses. "We understand how this product could be misinterpreted," said a spokesman, "and we respect that point of view."
Issue 501: March 5th

A grandfather who had his leg amputated three years ago has been told he must undergo a medical examination before his disabled parking permit can be renewed – in case his circumstances have changed. "I can assure them that my leg has not grown back," said Ron Craig, from Shipley in West Yorkshire. But Bradford Council is adamant: "We deal with all applications in the same way," said a spokesman.
Issue 514: June 4th 2005

A Dutch library has started lending people as well as books. As part of a drive to challenge stereotypes, visitors to Almelo public library can borrow gay people, gypsies and Muslims and talk to them for an hour about their lives. "Clients can borrow a Muslim woman in a headscarf and ask her questions they wouldn't dare to if they met on the street," explained library director Jan Krol.
Issue 526: August 27th 2005

Bald taxi drivers are to be purged from the Chinese city of Nanjing. Local authorities have proposed a ten-point plan to smarten up the city, and aesthetically displeasing cabbies are first on the list. Male taxi drivers have been told they cannot sport long hair, bald pates, moustaches or goatees, while female drivers must go easy on the make-up.
Issue 528: Sept 8th 2005

A French policeman has returned to work after spending 12 years on paternity leave. Despite being absent from police work for two-thirds of his career, Eric Krasker can now apply for promotion – to chief inspector. The father of five used his free time to become a world-renowned expert on the Beatles, and write two books about them.
Issue 533: Oct 15th 2005

It does take some of the magic out of it when they do that...

Crime Pays

A Washington DC drug operation had top be called off after an officer issued a press release – the day before the raid.
Issue 38: Feb 17th 1996

France's Most wanted criminal was finally arrested at Disneyland in Paris by undercover policemen disguised Mickey Mouse, Minnie Mouse and Daffy Duck.
Issue 44: March 30th 1996

Thieves are on the run after stealing 7,000 tablets for diarrhoea from a chemist in Watford, Herts.
Issue 49: May 4th 1996

A masked teenager held a New York chemist up at gunpoint and ordered him to fill up a paper bag with spot cream to treat his acne.
Issue 66: August 31st 1996

When Michael Manning, a Birmingham taxi firm owner, was attacked in his office by robbers with machetes, blood from his head soaked his VAT returns, forcing him to redo them. He has now been fined £3,000 for sending them in late.
Issue 67: Sept 7th 1996

A road safety engineer was booked by police for driving while operating a camcorder. He was making an accident prevention film in Crowthorne, Berks.
Issue 91: March 1st 1997

A blind man jailed for driving drunk through Louisville, Kentucky, claimed he was safe because his guide dog had been taught to bark once at a red light and twice at a green.
Issue 93: March 15th 1997

Paramajit Tatle, a Gloucester shopkeeper, scared off an armed robber by throwing sweets at him. The robber fired at Mrs Tatle but missed, and then fled under a shower of toffees and mints.
Issue 115: August 16th 1997

Hackers infiltrated the computerised switchboard of the New York Police Department and replaced the outgoing message with a new one that ran: "We're too busy eating doughnuts, drinking coffee and thinking about sex to take your call right now."
Issue 115: August 16th 1997

In Pori, Finland, serial litterers are made to stand in the place they littered for a whole day chanting "I am filthy", while wearing a plastic pig snout and ears. The scheme, devised by politician Arkus Fjarna, has already cut litter rates by 50 per cent. There is talk of extending it to fouling dog owners: "We'd make them wear a fake dog turd round their neck," said Mr Fjarna, "while chanting 'I am the owner of a dog that shits.'"
Issue 120: Sept 14th 1997

When a suspicious looking package was found outside a Territorial Army centre in Bristol, police blew it up, only to discover it had been full of leaflets on how to deal with suspicious packages.
Issue 121: Sept 21st 1997

Matsuo Kabishi, 47, an executive at Sappira Accountancy in Tokyo, has been arrested for attacking a male employee. She already had a reputation as a strict disciplinarian. During her six months with the firm Kabishi sacked one man for having dirty fingernails, stabbed another for crying because his mother had died, and set a secretary alight for making a typing error. Things came to a head when a trainee accountant broke wind during a meeting. Kabishi produced a cordless drill from her handbag and drilled him in the ear. She was arrested and fired.
Issue 123: Oct 11th 1997

Police called to a "road rage" incident at Southend in Essex, found a man wrecking his own car with a baseball bat after it ran out of petrol.
Issue 128: Nov 15th 1997

A driver was less than convincing when he drew up at public lavatories monitored by the police for indecent activities and told them he had stopped for a rest. Sgt Lester of Gloucester police said: "His story didn't hold water because he was wearing high-heeled shoes, fishnet stockings and a miniskirt."`
Issue 129: Nov 22nd 1997

During a rooftop protest at a Dublin detention centre, two 13-year-old young offenders outlined their demands: a personal audience with Pamela Anderson, a helicopter, £1,000 in cash, a bottle of orange juice and two cigarettes. The authorities refused to oblige, and both reprobates turned themselves in when their mothers showed up.
Issue 137: Jan 24th 1998

A Thai man has been jailed for 15 years for trying to have sex with an elephant. Kim Lee Chong, 61, was caught naked from the waist down, standing on a box behind the animal. He told the court the elephant was a reincarnation of his wife: "I recognised her immediately by the naughty glint in her eye."
Issue 139: Feb 7th 1998

Citizens of Montpellier, France, have suffered a spate of bag snatchings – all carried out by men on pogo sticks. "I was walking down the street when I heard a thudding sound behind me," recalled one woman. "I turned to see what it was and as I did two men bounced past on pogo sticks, one of them snatching my bag. I tried to chase them, but they were too fast." There have been nine such incidents, and in each case the robbers got away.
Issue 140: Feb 14th 1998

Six psychologists were arrested after falling out and brawling at a conference in Hamburg – on road rage.
Issue 147: April 4th 1998

A builder from Southampton has been dubbed the "Casanova conman", after he slept with 227 Norwegian girls and tricked them out of a fortune. David Coombs, 34, told The Sun he swindled £100,000 worth of money and jewellery from the "lonely beauties". Norwegian women are "fairly stupid", he says, "and with charm and good sex they open their handbags". After 63 complaints from Coombs's duped lovers, the Norwegian police have put his picture in all the papers, under the headline: "Impossible to get rid of."
Issue 151: May 2nd 1998

When Det. Constable Tim Crane of Bristol noticed how many cars were stopping outside the home of a suspected drug dealer, he asked the old lady living opposite to take down their registration numbers. When he returned a few days later, the old lady presented him with a pile of number plates. Taking his instructions literally, she had removed them from all of the cars.
Issue 167: August 22nd 1998

A kidnap attempt in Uruguay went spectacularly wrong when kidnapper Umberto Ciazza ended up being abducted himself. After breaking into the house of wealthy industrialist Cesar Platti and finding him not at home, Ciazza went into the master bedroom to await his return. Unfortunately another kidnapper, Alberto Prossas, was already hiding in the bedroom cupboard, and leapt out as soon as Ciazza entered the room. He forced a sack over his head, hustled him out of the house and held him prisoner for two days before realising his mistake. "We actually had a lot to talk about," admitted Ciazza. "We'd kidnapped many of the same people."
Issue 168: August 29th 1998

A prisoner in Utah has filed a $1m lawsuit for "emotional suffering" after state authorities suspended a programme which provided hair transplants for inmates.
Issue 168: August 29th 1998

A panty pincher has been arrested after stealing 10,000 pairs of knickers over a five-year period. The 37-year-old man was caught stripping a washing line while wearing a stolen swimming costume and someone else's pants. A room at his home in Wembley, London, was four feet deep in underpants.
Issue 171: Sept 19th 1998

Pennsylvania cops got a confession from a dim-witted crook by placing a sieve on his head and attaching it to a photocopier. Claiming it was a lie-detector, they put a sheet inside which read: "He's Lying". On seeing it, the criminal confessed.
Issue 175: Oct 17th 1998

Burglar Frank Gort broke down and sobbed when he was sentenced to seven years in jail, claiming it was his unlucky number.
An understanding judge in San Antonio, Texas, took pity and gave him eight years instead.
Issue 174: Oct 10th 1998

When raiders held up a bank in Rome, onlookers thought they were watching a film being made, and even applauded as the gang climbed onto motorbikes and fled with £200,000 worth of loot.
Issue 179: Nov 14th 1998

Albert Mantale, a 3ft 6in Ghanaian midget, was caned by the headmaster of a school he did not even attend. Mantale, 45, a black-board salesman, visited the school in Accra to drum up business. When he was shown into the headmaster's study he was mistaken for a pupil and given six of the best for not wearing a uniform. Despite his pleas, he was then made to stand in the corner for three hours. He is suing the school for assault.
Issue 185: Jan 2nd 1999

Four forgers were unmasked when they stuffed fake notes in the G-string of a stripper who was a bank clerk by day. "She called in the cops because the paper didn't feel right," said police in Oxnard, California. They were arrested as they left the Spearmint Rhino club near Santa Barbara, where they had been tipping heavily.
Issue 187: Jan 16th 1999

Drivers in Fort Lupton, Colorado who play their music too loud are fined £30 or made to listen to Barry Manilow records.
Issue 187: Jan 16th 1999

Mr Boyd of Bridlington was banned from driving after he ate an out-of-date tax disc in front of police so they'd have no evidence to prosecute him. As officers approached the car, he stuffed the disc into his mouth and said: "It's gone, mate."
Issue 189: Jan 30th 1999

Police are chasing a woman who goes into flower shops in Istanbul, Turkey, eats 24 roses and then flees without paying.
Issue 195: March 13th 1999

Lonely Olga Karpov has been arrested in Moscow for causing eight accidents by hurling herself under the cars of good-looking drivers. "I thought that one of the men might ask me out to make up for it," said Olga.
Issue 197: March 27th 1999

In Muswell Hill, London, truancy patrol officer Sergeant Richard Watling pounced on a suspected truant and demanded: "Now then young man, what school do you go to?" "I am not a young man," came the reply. "I am a lady. And I don't go to school because I am 38."
Issue 202: May 1st 1999

Sales manager Rene Joly, of Toronto, Canada, went to court claiming that the defence minister and several drugstore chains conspired to kill him because he is a Martian. The judge dismissed his case on the grounds that, as a Martian, he has no status before the courts.
Issue 206: May 29th 1999

Bank robbers who tried to blow a safe in Malaysia demolished the entire building, leaving only the safe intact.
Issue 210: June 26th 1999

Inept car thief Lee Hoskens took pictures of himself stealing a Vauxhall Astra with a camera he found in the glove compartment. Lee and his girlfriend took turns posing, before crashing the car and fleeing from the scene, leaving the camera behind as evidence. "It's amazing just how stupid some criminals can be," said a spokesman for Somerset and Avon Police.
Issue 215: July 31st 1999

When customs officers in Sweden searched a suspiciously busty woman arriving from Denmark they found 67 snakes and six lizards hidden in her bra. The woman claimed she was planning to start a reptile farm.
Issue 215: July 31st 1999

When the police raided a party in Leicester, a drunken reveller tried to flee in a 7mph milk float. Three officers walked briskly behind the float to catch up with him. Matthew North, 23, who had lost his licence for driving a steamroller when drunk, was jailed for six months.
Issue 217: August 14th 1999

Jackie Cruickshank, 30, a single mother from Shoeburyness, Essex, has had her house broken into four times by the same burglar. The crook sneaks in when she is out, unloads the dishwasher, does the vacuuming and dusts the furniture. "It is nice to get the housework done," Jackie said, "but it's a bit sinister."
Issue 218: August 21st 1999

A drug trafficker under house arrest in Florence begged police to put him in prison because his wife and mother-in-law were driving him mad. Paolo Palvotti, 29, was given an eight-year term at home to save the state money. But after three years he begged: "Please put me in jail. They're driving me to an early grave with their nagging."
Issue 222: Sept 18th 1999

US judges cut the jail term of robber Barry Kemp, 33, of Louisville, Kentucky, from 3,045 to 1,045 years on the basis that it was "too harsh".
Issue 222: Sept 18th 1999

A thief who steals milk from Anna Ryder's doorstep in St Leonards-on-Sea has left a note asking if she can possible order semi-skimmed in future.
Issue 223: Sept 25th 1999

Magistrates in Swaffam, Norfolk, have jailed a man who threatened to kill his social worker, reported the Eastern Daily Press. The man was enraged by delays in arranging his anger management course.
Issue 225: Oct 9th 1999

A "private citizen" who volunteered to make love to prostitutes in order to trap them for the police has received £4,000 in fees and been praised for his "marvellous sense of public duty" in Edmonton, Canada.
Issue 228: Oct 30th 1999

A policeman was forced to resign after sleeping with both the victim and the perpetrator of a handbag robbery, reports The Sun. PC Mark Tims, 32, of Banbury, Oxfordshire, arrested a 16-year-old for the theft, handcuffed her and then romped with her in the police car. Later he seduced the 18-year-old robbery victim, Helena Jones, after calling at her home to offer crime prevention advice. When the girls confronted him after discovering his duplicity, he suggested they have a threesome.
Issue 231: Nov 20th 1999

A dress made of 48 dollar bills stitched together and designed to depict the sin of greed, was stolen from an exhibition in St Paul, Minnesota, US.
Issue 231: Nov 20th 1999

An increasing number of Sicilian Mafia hitmen are seeking psychiatric help. "Killers worry that they are not brave enough or that they lack self-confidence in social situations," says a University of Palermo report.
Issue 232: Nov 27th 1999

French thieves dumped a lorry load of cheap wine outside Paris, with a note saying: "We're not drinking this rubbish."
Issue 233: Dec 4th 1999

A priest caught speeding at 120mph told a court his car had been "possessed by evil". Father Philippe Laguiere, 52, told a judge in Bordeaux, France: "The accelerator went down on its own. I can only assume some evil force took over." He was banned for six months.
Issue 234: Dec 11th 1999

A motorist caught by a speed camera near Denver decided to respond in kind, mailing a photograph of two $20 bills to pay his $40 fine. He paid up real cash after the police sent him, by return of post, a photo of a pair of handcuffs.
Issue 243: Feb 19th 2000

It is legal to kill a Welshman, according to a recently uncovered 1,000-year-old law. But only in Hereford's Cathedral Close on a Sunday with a longbow from exactly 12 yards. Catrin Harries of the Wales Tourist Board, said: "We're not bracing ourselves for a flood of attacks."
Issue 244: Feb 26th 2000

A former SAS soldier accused of assaulting four police officers appeared in court in Maidstone this week dressed as a woman. John White, a six-foot-two Gulf War veteran who prefers to be called Joanna, wore a bright red hat, purple dress, earrings, necklace and mauve lipstick. Clutching a cuddly toy, he denied claims that he had tossed the police officers around "like rag dolls" as they struggled to handcuff him during an incident in a pub.
Issue 248: March 25th 2000

Police trying to help an elderly couple locked out of their car had a stroke of luck when two known joyriders walked past. The bobbies asked the villains to ply their trade on the Vauxhall Astra, which they did – in eight seconds. The couple, from Exmouth in Devon, gave the thieves £1 each for their help.
Issue 249: April 1st 2000

A football team of Yorkshire policemen was trailing 2-0 until an eagle-eyed copper spotted a wanted man in the opposing team. The villain was promptly arrested, enabling the forces of law and order to surge ahead for a 3-2 win.
Issue 251: April 15th 2000

Inventor Chris Goodland, 43, who won an award for a thief-proof lock, had his design work stolen from his home in Bridport, Dorset.
Issue 254: May 6th 2000

Colombian police who raided the country's largest all-male jail were surprised to find the prison also contained 511 women, a sauna, a gym, drugs, distilleries and dogs. The national police chief described Modelo jail as a hotbed of corruption and prostitution.
Issue 255: May 13th 2000

Yousef Khishen stole two wallets while handcuffed to a cop on a bus in Damascus, Syria. He had been arrested for pickpocketing.
Issue 257: May 27th 2000

A smoker from Charlotte, North Carolina, bought a box of expensive cigars and insured them against, among other things, fire. A month later, having smoked the cigars, he made a claim saying they were lost in a "series of small fires". When the insurer refused to pay, he sued and the insurance company had to cough up $15,000. No sooner had the smoker cashed the cheque, however, than he was arrested on 24 counts of arson. He was then convicted of intentionally burning his own property, fined $24,000 and sent to jail.
Issue 258: June 3rd 2000

Judges in Saudi Arabia have sentenced a Filipino man to 75 lashes for possession of alcohol after he was caught with two chocolate liqueurs at an airport.
Issue 259: June 10th 2000

Dentist Theodoros Vassiliadis, 54, has been jailed for four years in Athens for using screws from his television set to fix false teeth.
Issue 259: June 10th 2000

After a community centre in Croydon was repeatedly burgled, staff tacked a sign to the door reading: "Nothing left to steal." A thief broke in anyway – and left a note saying: "Just checking!"
Issue 270: August 26th 2000

A policeman knocked himself out while searching a clothes shop in the Wirral, Mersey-side. The hapless copper rugby-tackled what he thought was an intruder – and hit a long mirror head first.
Issue 273: Sept 16th 2000

A car thief was caught in Hammersmith, west London, when he tried to break into an unmarked van which police were using as a surveillance vehicle.
Issue 275: Sept 30th 2000

When Los Angeles patrolman Jason Furund saw a 19-year-old youth snatching an old woman's bag, he leapt out of his car and gave chase. Realising he had no chance of catching him, Furund began to bark loudly – at which point the felon skidded to a halt, raised his hands to the air and begged the officer to call off his dog.
Issue 276: Oct 7th 2000

Thieves raiding a house in Essex snorted the ashes of a dead dog after mistaking a bag of powder – marked 'Charlie' – for a stash of cocaine. "It was horrible knowing they were in my house," said Dee Blyth, "but the idea of them trying to get high on a dead dog certainly made me feel better."
Issue 278: Oct 21st 2000

A thief in Oslo broke into a flat, unaware that it was being used for the Norwegian version of the Big Brother TV show. The man grabbed £500 in cash and a bottle of perfume before realising that 17 cameras were trained on him. He was immediately arrested.
Issue 281: Nov 11th 2000

An inmate who accidentally shot himself is suing New York prison chiefs for $5 million for allowing him to smuggle a gun into his cell.
Issue 282: Nov 18th 2000

A suspect gave himself away during an identity parade in Los Angeles when police ordered him to repeat the phrase "Give me your money or I shoot." "Hey, that's not what I said," blurted the thief.
Issue 284: Dec 2nd 2000

Police in Maiduguri, northern Nigeria, are pursuing a witch doctor who turned a schoolboy into a yam. Mala Kachalla, an official working for the governor of Borno state, said: "There has been a strange incident." The vegetable has been locked in a cell for its own protection.
Issue 288: Dec 30th 2000

A Lebanese man evaded Israeli border security by trampolining over a fence. Border guards did not notice that Anton Shizar had bounced into the country until he was arrested 60 miles south of the border.
Issue 291: Jan 27th 2001

A gang of female thieves in Durban, South Africa, got away with robbing over 100 shops by stripping naked whenever police tried to chase them. Police spokesman Ronnie Winter explained: "We knew what the consequences might have been if we had tried arresting naked women."
Issue 294: Feb 17th 2001

Two burglars were arrested after falling asleep during a job. A man arriving at his home in Cardiff was puzzled to find his possessions stacked neatly by the front door. When he went upstairs he discovered a man and a woman fast asleep on his bed.
Issue 296: March 3rd 2001

A 23-year-old Ugandan on trial for trespassing on a burial site cited his insatiable desire for human meat as his defence. "We are a family of cannibals," Ssande Sserwadda told the court in Luweero. "I feel queasy if I go too long without human meat. But just because we eat human flesh, does that mean we're bad people?" On being sentenced to three years in prison, Sserwadda asked if he could take with him the human leg bone that had earlier been used as an exhibit. "It's a shame to let it go to waste," he said.
Issue 305: May 5th 2001

A woman of 76 who remained silent when repeatedly questioned by a Detroit judge was found to be dead in the court room.
Issue 308: May 26th 2001

Three female thieves have been arrested in Bogota, Colombia, after local police discovered they were preying on men by smearing their breasts with a powerful drug and enticing their victims to lick them. The women stood by the side of the road, striking seductive poses to lure male drivers to stop and feast on their breasts. Once their victims were unconscious they stole their wallets and their cars.
Issue 311: June 16th 2001

Scotland Yard is holding an inquiry into a complaint that a detective broke wind during a raid in Chingford, Essex, and failed to apologise. The complaint is being handled by the force's internal disciplinary body.
Issue 311: June 16th 2001

A young woman caught speeding at 105mph told police she was in a hurry to get home to make love to her husband, having not had sex for 48 hours. "When I need to have it, I need to have it," said Claire Warburton, 29. She was fined £200 by magistrates in Harrogate.
Issue 315: July 14th 2001

An Oregon car dealer has been fined £80,000 for selling seven sports cars in a month to a 78-year-old Alzheimer's sufferer who doesn't drive.
Issue 322: Sept 21st 2001

Jeremy Locock, 29, of Blandford, Dorset, was jailed for a month for swiping his probation officer's wallet as they discussed his community service.
Issue 322: Sept 21st 2001

A teenager who tried to rob a bus in Chile was horrified to discover that his mother was among the passengers. The boy, along with two of his friends, was threatening the driver with knives and a baseball bat when he heard a familiar voice telling him to stop it at once, and ordering him off the bus.
Issue 323: Sept 8th 2001

A motorist in Petersfield was so taken with the traffic warden that issued him with a ticket for parking illegally until she agreed to go out with him. Colin O'Neill and Doris Lemon have now married. "She's so pretty, I fell for her straight away," said Colin.
Issue 324: Sept 15th 2001

A man has been arrested after applying to join the police in Baltimore. Asked whether he had ever committed a crime, Edwin Gaynor ticked the box marked "yes". When questioned, he admitted to hijacking a car and robbing five people in Texas.
Issue 324: Sept 15th 2001

An unemployed Californian man has been arrested after making four telephone calls to a tower block in Los Angeles warning that it was about to be destroyed. He told police that he made the threats so that a friend who worked in the building would get the day off. Meanwhile in Canada, police were called to a public lavatory after a suspicious white powder was spotted on a baby-changing mat. "The chances are that it's going to be baby powder," said an officer in Toronto.
Issue 330: Oct 27th 2001

A motorist in Lincolnshire has been ordered to stop waving a sign that says "Naff git!" at drivers with personalised number plates. Unemployed trucker Paul Reed, 40, received a police warning after complaints from drivers with special plates. "The fact that these ridiculous motorists complained has made my point perfectly," said Reed. "They take themselves far too seriously and have no sense of humour."
Issue 332: Nov 10th 2001

A passenger was arrested at Miami airport after customs officials found 44 songbirds hidden in his trousers. Carlos Avila was rumbled when a vigilant airport inspector asked him to roll up his trousers and saw a Cuban Singing Finch strapped to his leg. Avila has been charged with unlawful importation.
Issue 334: Nov 24th 2001

A man who robbed an Iowa convenience store came back to retrieve his wallet, found the shopkeeper on the phone describing him to police and started correcting his facts. "He's about 5ft 10," the shop-keeper was saying. "I'm 6ft 2," the suspect huffed. "And about 38 years old," the shopkeeper continued. "I'm 34," protested the suspect. A deputy sheriff arrived moments later to arrest him.
Issue 335: Dec 1st 2001

Police in Lancashire have sent Christmas cards to more than 600 suspected burglars with the message: "Happy Christmas – We're Going to Catch You".
Issue 337: Dec 15th 2001

A puppet of Osama bin Laden was arrested by army officers during New Year celebrations in La Calera, north of Bogota. The arresting officers described the puppet's uniform as "suspicious", and demanded to check its plastic firearm. The puppet was taken to a nearby military base and thoroughly frisked before being returned to the party.
Issue 340: Jan 12th 2002

Angelica Flores and her husband were arrested, handcuffed and jailed for failing to take down the Christmas lights on their Arizona home by the local council deadline.
Issue 345: Feb 16th 2002

Michael Marcum, 21, has been found guilty of stealing six 350-pound electrical transformers from a power company in Stanberry, Missouri. He wanted to build a time machine so he could transport himself a few days into the future, learn the winning lottery numbers, and return to buy the right ticket.
Issue 345: Feb 16th 2002

A Romanian pensioner is facing jail after falling asleep while listening to a telephone sex line. Constantin Lucien ran up a bill of £950 – equivalent to a year's pay in Romania. He has refused to pay, arguing: "It was boring."
Issue 346: Feb 23rd 2002

A Texan who has been charged with attempted murder claims that he is the victim of a rare condition in which homicidal anger is triggered by certain words. Thomas Mitchell says he could not help shooting his ex-girlfriend because he was sure she was about to say "New Jersey". The words "Snickers", "Mars Bar" and "Wisconsin" have a similar effect on him. Officials at the court in Galveston were so afraid of a repeat performance they used flash cards rather than speak the fateful words.
Issue 346: Feb 23rd 2002

Susan Wallace, 47, has been charged with assault after throwing her iguana at a pub doorman and a police officer. Wallace had been annoying fellow drinkers at the Anchor Inn in Cowes by placing Igwig, a green tree lizard, on their heads. When the doorman tried to intervene, she threw Igwig at his head. And when PC David Harry tried to arrest her for criminal damage, she threw the creature at him too. "It crawled up my back, right up to my ear," he told the court. "I was a little concerned."

Issue 347: March 2nd 2002

A man who threatened serious harm with a cream pastry has been given two years' probation by a Tees-side court. Craig Cockerell, 21, was making off with a haul of cakes he had stolen from Kwik Save in Stockton when he was spotted by a security guard. After a chase, he rounded on his pursuer. "I'm not going back with you," he said, pulling a weapon from his back pocket. It was a cream horn.

Issue 352: April 6th 2002

Two policemen have been suspended in Calcutta after one of them bit the hand of a lorry driver who refused to pay him a bribe.

Issue 353: April 13th 2002

A Michigan court recently heard evidence from the world's worst hijacker. The unnamed defendant was on an internal flight from New York when he leapt to his feet, pulled a gun out of his pocket and screamed, "Take me to Detroit or you're all going to f***ing die!" When an air steward pointed out, "Er, we are going to Detroit," he put his gun away, sat down in a huff, and was silent for the remainder of the flight. He was arrested as he got off the plane.

Issue 357: May 11th 2002

A 22-year-old American man from Gary, Indiana, has been arrested and charged with shooting his best friend during an argument over which of the two was the better friend.

Issue 359: May 25th 2002

A German man has been charged with causing bodily harm after he attacked a policeman with his underpants. The 23-year-old was arrested while travelling on a train without a ticket, and taken to a police station at Hanau. On arrival, he suddenly ripped off his clothes and beat one officer around the face with his underpants.

Issue 362: June 15th 2002

Two men accused of eating human body parts have been freed by a Cambodian provincial court because there is no specific law against cannibalism. The two men, both crematorium workers, were arrested for eating fingers and toes from a body they were cremating. "I ordered the military police to release them late Friday because there is no law to charge them with," said Nhou Tholsaid, a public prosecutor.
Issue 363: June 22nd 2002

A drunken fight between two Florida fishermen ended when one of them used their catch of the day as a weapon. Garth Spacek, 42, is recovering in hospital after being stabbed with the bill of a swordfish.
Issue 364: June 29th 2002

A Thai man was drugged and robbed after sucking the sedative-coated nipples of two pretty women. Nontakorn Pearsontea, 27, was waiting at a bus stop in the city of Nakorn when the women approached him, removed their tops and invited him to suck their breasts. "I could not refuse but I woke up and found I had lost everything," he said.
Issue 365: July 6th 2002

Rich Americans have come up with a novel form of excitement: designer kidnaps. For a few hundred dollars, organisers will discuss your preferred type of abduction. Then, a few days later, masked men will drag you into the back of a van, and keep you captive for the agreed period. Organiser Brock Enright has conducted 24 such kidnappings; one client asked to be shoved into a hole and forced to stay there for days.
Issue 369: August 3rd 2002

An Italian boss has been arrested for charging an illegal immigrant rent to live in a car. The 35-year-old Tunisian refugee was found living in an old estate car which had been decorated with a bed, small desk and TV. "I was happy there and really thought I could settle down," he said.
Issue 371: August 17th 2002

Nigerian police are investigating a claim that a boy has been turned into a yam by a witch doctor. Three schoolboys swore their friend had been changed into a vegetable before their very eyes after accepting sweets from a stranger. A large yam has been taken into custody for further investigation.
Issue 372: August 24th 2002

Police are searching for a female driver who whizzed along the motorway while eating a steak-and-chip dinner with a knife and fork. Drivers on the M27 reported a woman driving erratically, and upon closer inspection, saw her carving up her steak with cutlery from a plate balanced on her lap.
Issue 373: August 31st 2002

A Bangladeshi village which is populated entirely by thieves has been cordoned off by police. In a recent Bangladeshi census, the residents of Jahanpur all listed their occupation as "thief". The police have now set up a ring of guards around the village to contain the problem. "These people do not know about any other means of livelihood," said a police spokesman.
Issue 376: Sept 21st 2002

America's most organised bank robber has been caught by police. New York coppers were performing a routine stop-and-search on a motorist when they came across an unusual to-do list. The note read: "Drive to Maine. Get safer place to stay. Buy guns. Get car. Rob bank. Go to New York."
Issue 379: Oct 12th 2002

The world's most accident-prone bank robber has struck in Miami. The hapless criminal had just finished collecting his loot when he put his gun in his pocket too hastily and shot himself in the leg. Staggering towards his getaway car, he tripped on the pavement and knocked out two of his gold teeth. After struggling to his feet he crossed the road, only to be run down by a van. Police are looking for a man with a bullet in his leg, two missing teeth and serious head wounds.
Issue 380: Oct 19th 2002

A Berlin traffic policeman has been suspended from duty for allowing an attractive 22-year-old blonde to pay off her speeding fine by kissing him for an hour.
Issue 387: Dec 7th 2002

An armed robber who raided an Argentinian petrol station more than 100 times has been hired as its head of security. "After having robbed us so many times, he knows everything about the gas station," explained owner Andres Pietro. "Besides, if I have to give him money every month under a gun menace, I prefer to have him working for me."
Issue 391: Jan 11th 2003

A Mafia hitman who is standing trial for murder in Sicily has produced the perfect alibi – he was busy killing two other men at the time. Salvatore Torre, 33, told the Italian court he couldn't possibly have gunned down gang rivals Luigi Sano and Bartolo Milone 11 years ago. "I am not the killer," he said. "In fact, I committed another crime that day, of which no-one has accused me: the murders of Sebastiano Montagno Campagnolo and Antonino Anastasi."
Issue 392: Jan 18th 2003

A Yorkshire cocaine dealer has been jailed for three years after boasting about his occupation on the Friends Reunited website. Police caught up with Raymond Casling, 24, after he posted a message to old school-friends reading: "I'm doing very well. I'm selling a lot of charlie in Redcar and I've got three sports cars."
Issue 392: Jan 18th 2003

A Japanese man drove his car through a train station in a bid to get noticed. After dropping a friend off at Yamagata station, Masafumi Saito, 20, shouted hello to a passing women. When she ignored him, he drove his car up a 65-foot flight of stairs, around the main concourse, through a corridor and down another flight of stairs trying to get her attention. Police have charged him with wilful destruction of property.
Issue 392: Jan 18th 2003

A Romanian driver has been fined £10 – the equivalent of a week's wages – after failing to slow down while passing a rabbit. A police spokesman explained: "A rabbit today, a child tomorrow."
Issue 395: Feb 8th 2003

A Kentucky man was arrested after he turned his entire house into a bong. William Hainline put a huge mound of marijuana on to a barbecue next to his open window, and then placed a fan at the other end of the house, which sucked all the smoke into the front room – where his 52nd birthday party was taking place. "It was the biggest bong we'd ever seen," said an officer.
Issue 396: Feb 15th 2003

New Zealand police have apprehended the country's most dangerous driver. Last week they pulled over a naked man who was speeding down the road on a motorised bar stool with flames streaming from a rolled-up newspaper jammed between his buttocks. He has been charged with driving an unlicensed vehicle.
Issue 398: March 1st 2003

Police in Chile have arrested a bank robber with no arms or legs. The man drove the getaway car for a gang that robbed a Santiago bank. He told police that he learned to drive using a Formula 1 simulator, and managed to control the getaway car by tying his knees to the steering wheel and operating the pedals with sticks that he'd tied to his elbows. Police have commended him for his bravery.
Issue 399: March 8th 2003

Austrian police raided several bakeries across the country after receiving a tip-off that their doughnuts did not contain enough jam. And so it turned out: in every third doughnut tested by police, the jam content was less than the required 15%. Dozens of bakers are now facing court charges and, if found guilty, could spend three months in jail for fraud.
Issue 399: March 8th 2003

A nativity scene made of pure cocaine has been seized by Italian customs officials. Airport officials in Rome were suspicious when they saw the 3kg parcel from Peru. On closer examination, they discovered that the manger, figures, ox and donkey had all been carved out of blocks of pure cocaine – and that the nativity scene was worth £1m. The owner, a 50-year-old man from Rome, described it as "a unique artwork from South America".
Issue 404: April 12th 2003

A Texan man has filed a £170,000 lawsuit against himself for making his own life a misery. His lawyer explained that the man is suffering from a multiple-personality disorder. Six of his characters are respectable citizens, but the seventh is a drunken bully. If he wins his case his own insurance company will have to pay out.
Issue 407: May 3rd 2003

Louisiana police are looking for a kind, clean burglar. The intruder keeps breaking into houses in the town of Mandeville and taking a shower, leaving behind a basket of fresh strawberries and £30 cash. "It's still a crime," said a policeman. "We must stop him before he intrudes, bathes and drops money again."
Issue 407: May 3rd 2003

A group of thieves in Gloucestershire left a trail straight to their door after stealing a safe and dragging it for a mile behind their car. Villagers in Cam called police after being awoken by the sound of the one-ton steel box rattling down the high street. Officers followed the gouges in the road and found the safe sitting outside the suspects' flat. "It wasn't our greatest piece of detective work," said a spokesman.
Issue 411: May 31st 2003

A suspect from Tennessee gave himself up in terror when a policeman growled at him. John Hood, 21, fled into a forest after his car was pulled over by Deputy Sheriff Henry Ritter. When Hood refused to come out, Ritter pretended to be a sniffer dog prowling towards him, barking and growling. Hood immediately surrendered, begging him to call off the dog. "I had no plans to bite the suspect," said Ritter.
Issue 419: July 26th 2003

The police had no trouble apprehending a gang of thieves who stole booze from Walton-on-Thames football club. The robbers made their escape on a pitch-marking machine, but forgot to switch off the line-painting mechanism. The cops simply followed the white line and nabbed them.

Issue 420: August 2nd 2003

Police have criticised the hygiene standards at a motel in Kansas after cleaners failed to notice a man, clad in fishnet stockings and a wimple, lying dead in one of the rooms. "The Capri has been closed in the past for indecency and poor hygiene," said Sergeant Darin Snapp. "On the other hand, it is a competitively priced motel with many facilities, including a pool table and a gym."

Issue 424: August 30th 2003

A Michigan student is paying his way through nursing school by selling "bullet-hole stickers" so that wannabe criminals can pretend their car has been the target of a drive-by shooting. Doug Rock's website, bullet1.com, features .50 and .22 calibre bullet holes. "Now you can have the best parts of being in a gang without any collateral damage," says the blurb. "Cruise the streets in style, knowing that all the real gangstas are envying you."

Issue 432: Oct 25th 2003

A convicted murderer is hoping for a fresh start, after serving a 99-year sentence. Frenchman Jean Dupont was jailed for killing his mother's lover in 1904, when he was just 14. Now 113, he says: "I'm ready to make up for lost time. I hope to find a wife and have children in the years I have left."

Issue 433: Nov 1st 2003

Two women in Tampa, Florida, foiled an armed robber by plying him with rum until he passed out. Cathy Ord, 60, and Rose Bucher, 63, decided to try to befriend the robber, Alfred Joseph Sweet, after he burst through their kitchen window brandishing a sawn-off shotgun. They made him a ham sandwich, gave him a bottle of rum and suggested he have a shower and a shave to make himself less recognisable to the police. After five hours of their kindly ministrations, 52-year-old Sweet nodded off. He was still slumbering when the police arrived to arrest him.

Issue 434: Nov 8th 2003

A Finnish bank manager foiled a robbery by persuading the three perpetrators to take out a loan instead. The robbers, who were all drunk and in their fifties, burst into the bank at Haukivuoir, near Helsinki, and demanded €50,000. But the branch manager suggested that a loan would be more sensible all round. He offered them a €10 cash advance and told them to return in ten minutes to sign the loan papers. They were arrested in their homes before they could get back to the bank.
Issue 435: Nov 15th 2003

A New Zealand motorist with the number plate 2DRUNK, has been convicted of drink driving for a second time. Judge Stephen O'Driscoll said Philip Bain, 33, was "just asking" to be stopped.
Issue 436: Nov 22nd 2003

An armed robber was caught after he dropped his mobile phone at the crime scene. Police in Detroit used the phone to ring Wilbert Boswell at home and invite him down to the station to collect it. When the 49-year-old turned up, he was duly nicked. "When you're dealing with criminals at this level, you find they aren't very sharp," said a police spokesman.
Issue 438: Dec 6th 2003

Three German schoolboys who went on an internet shopping spree spent £85m on a stolen credit card. The 19-year-old boys, who had just completed an IT course, hacked into the credit card account of an unsuspecting man from Ludwisburg, and bought aeroplanes, country estates, restaurants and paintings during their lunch break, before police arrested them at their grammar school in Hesse.
Issue 440: Dec 20th 2003

A German shoplifter was so seized with guilt that he posted his haul to the police to return to the shops. The robber also enclosed letters to the heads of each store, apologising and advising them on how to improve security. The parcel was posted to Darmstadt police station, with the sender's address given as: "Mea Culpa, 1 Honest Street".
Issue 441: Dec 27th 2003

A Colombian man came up with a novel idea for a burglary – he hid in a box and posted himself to the house of a rich man. But the owner of the Medellin house became suspicious at the size of the package, and called in the bomb squad. When the thief burst out of the box wielding a knife, he found himself surrounded by police.
Issue 443: Jan 17th 2004

A saleswoman in a Bosnian crockery shop thwarted a robbery by hurling plates at the thieves. Vahida Kadric hid behind the counter when masked gunmen burst into the store in Zenica, and then started lobbing plates at their heads. She got through an entire dinner set before they fled. "Fortunately," she said, "it was not one of our more expensive lines."
Issue 445: Jan 31st 2004

A beggar in the Czech Republic has been arrested after disguising himself as a water nymph to con young skaters. The 47-year-old – who was dressed in a green fairy costume covered in green ribbons – told children skating on a lake in Brno that the ice would break unless they gave him their pocket money. "Nobody is allowed to beg in Brno," said a police spokesman. "Not even water sprites."
Issue 446: Feb 7th 2004

A Tokyo undertaker has been arrested after murdering his aunt because he needed the business. Nobuhiko Takahashi, 42, beat his Aunt Chiyoko to death with a golf club because trade was slow. "I thought I would be able to undertake a funeral if I killed Auntie," he told police. The plan failed – a rival firm was given the job.
Issue 448: Feb 21st 2004

A New Orleans man was arrested after complaining to police that he had been sold dud crack cocaine. Joseph Bulot, 32, told an officer that he had swapped his micro-wave for the crack, but it hadn't made him high. He even handed in his crack pipe for analysis: tests showed that he had indeed been ripped off – there was no trace of cocaine in the pipe – but he was arrested anyway for possession of drug paraphernalia.
Issue 450: March 6th 2004

A hit and run driver who ran over a policeman in Romania turned out to be a deaf, blind pensioner. Aurel Blidaru, 84, was on his way to collect his pension when he hit the officer in the western town of Timisoara. Unaware of the incident, he left the policeman lying in the road with a broken leg, and drove off with police cars in hot pursuit. Officers couldn't believe it when he finally climbed out of the car wearing dark glasses and carrying a white stick. "I've been driving since 1950 and I've never had any problems," says Mr Blidaru, who has been stripped of his licence. "I am registered as deaf and blind, but can still see a bit out of one eye, and I know the route to the bank."
Issue 453: March 27th 2004

A pensioner who was driving the wrong way down a motorway stopped when he saw the police – to complain about the other motorists. "I'm glad to see you. There are all these drivers going the wrong way," said the 86-year-old from Bern, Switzerland. He said he had even flashed his lights at six motorists to alert them to their mistake. The officers confiscated the grandfather's licence and drove him home.
Issue 456: April 17th 2004

A Dutch woman was briefly £246m richer, after her local benefit office made a clerical error. Yolanda Schaap, 39, couldn't believe her eyes when she saw her bank balance, as she was only expecting her dole of £24. The office in Ulft, near Arnheim, swiftly rectified the mistake – but she didn't mind. "A couple of thousand would have been nice," she says, "but I wouldn't have known what to do with all those millions. It would have only brought about envy."
Issue 457: April 24th 2004

A Canadian motorist has been charged with careless driving after police caught him playing the violin at the wheel. The 54-year-old protested that he was warming up for a concert in which he was playing, but police charged him anyway. "It was lucky he didn't play the cello," said an officer.
Issue 457: April 24th 2004

An American pensioner suspected of fraud has lost her attorney after writing him a bad cheque. Betty Gooch, 75, who walks with a frame and carries oxygen with her, was charged with five counts of theft by deception after scamming a dozen car dealers. "She gave me this sob story", says Stephen Ford, who has stepped down as her lawyer. "She gave me a cheque for a retainer and I took it." Mrs Gooch is on the run, having missed a court hearing in Woodstock, Illinois.
Issue 458: May 1st 2004

A Filipino lawyer has told a court that the drugs found in his client's hen coop belonged to the birds. Manuel Urbina claims that the defendant, Francisco Armando Rivera, didn't own the 67kg of cocaine or the gun that were both found in the cage. "The drugs were in the possession of a rooster and two hens," he says, "and the law is clear that whoever is in possession of the drugs is the one who should be accused."
Issue 458: May 1st 2004

A teacher from Brooklyn, New York, has been suspended after hanging a five-year-old child from a coat-rack in the staffroom. Jason Schoenberger, 24, said he wanted to surprise a fellow teacher.
Issue 463: June 5th 2004

More than 50 police officers in Nogales, Mexico, were detained after work because someone had been making frog noises on the emergency radio. When no one owned up, the officers were kept back for eight hours as a punishment. "We had to send the message that such pranks won't be tolerated," said a spokesman.
Issue 464: June 6th 2004

Thieves who stole a portaloo in Gomel, Belarus, accidentally kidnapped a man who was using it at the time. The robbers loaded the lavatory on to their tractor trailer and drove off. The bemused 45-year-old man sitting inside opened the door to find himself being driven at high speed through the suburbs. He jumped out and went to police, who later discovered the missing lavatory during a raid on a private home.
Issue 465: June 19th 2004

A would-be cat burglar who broke into an art gallery through a skylight and lowered himself down a rope was forced to call the police for assistance when he couldn't climb back up again. CCTV footage from the Saper Galleries in East Lansing, Michigan, shows the robber trying unsuccessfully to clamber back up the rope, before using the gallery's own telephone to call the police. "There are professional thieves, but this guy was a total loser," said gallery owner Roy Saper.
Issue 470: July 24th 2004

A traffic policeman in the Czech city of Plezen has been suspended for shooting at disobedient pedestrians. The officer fired over the pedestrians' heads because they crossed the road while the light was red. One of the bullets hit the side of a car, but no one was hurt.
Issue 471: July 31st 2004

If you're going to rob a bank don't rent your getaway car from a hire company. That was the lesson learnt by a brother and sister team who held up a branch of Credit Union in Council Bluffs, Nebraska, and inadvertently dropped their rental agreement at the crime scene. It stated that the car was due back at 6pm. The police turned up on the hour, as did the robbers who were caught red-handed, the cash and guns on the back seat.
Issue 475: August 28th 2004

An Indian army officer who won a medal for bravery has been sacked, after it turned out that he had merely splashed ketchup on civilians and pretended they were dead rebels. A court martial found that photographs of dead Assamese separatists, supposedly killed by Colonel H.S. Kohli in a gun battle, actually showed members of his civilian staff covered in ketchup, lying very still.
Issue 479: Sept 25th 2004

Police in Russia are investigating a pensioner who killed a stranger with a courgette. When a drunken man broke into his apartment, the 62-year-old grabbed the vegetable, which he had grown on his allotment, and whacked the intruder on the head, killing him instantly.
Issue 482: Oct 16th 2004

Austrian police have caught a man who was terrorising elderly hikers by leaping out of bushes dressed as a gorilla. The prankster struck dozens of times in the scenic area of Neusiedlersee-Hügelland before police armed with tranquiliser guns managed to apprehend him. The 25-year-old local said the place was so boring he just wanted to give people something to talk about. He was released on bail after handing over the gorilla suit.
Issue 484: Oct 30th 2004

A Singapore judge was so enraged when a prosecution witness yawned in the middle of a trial that he sentenced him to two years' hard labour. Ng Jun Yee was waiting to testify in the trial of a man accused of stealing a scythe when he let out the yawn. "I am so sorry we are boring you," said Judge Li Do Joon. "Perhaps you will find it more interesting smashing rocks with a sledgehammer?"
Issue 485: Nov 6th 2004

A blind man in Lithuania was so annoyed when his friends called him useless that he decided to steal a car to prove them wrong. Alin Popescu, 24, broke into the parked car, started the ignition using a screwdriver and drove for half a mile down a busy road before crashing. "I only crashed because I was not sure of the route home," he told police.
Issue 485: Nov 6th 2004

Australian police are claiming the record for the longest car chase after pursuing a vehicle for 373 miles. They didn't exactly catch it: they simply shut all the petrol stations on the route, and waited for the thieves to run out of fuel.
Issue 488: Nov 27th 2004

A man has been arrested in Russia for peeing in a shop's display lavatory. Staff at the store in Kirov, west Russia, suddenly noticed the man unzip his trousers and urinate in the lavatory in the middle of the showroom. "I assumed customers would be allowed to try out the products before buying them," he told police.
Issue 490: Dec 11th 2004

Kevin Winston was determined to teach his 16-year-old daughter a lesson when she came home drunk, so he called the police. Big mistake. When the cops arrived at their house in New Jersey, the girl led them straight to a secret space in the roof, where her father had hidden his AK47, a sawn off shotgun and 617 vials of cocaine.
Issue 491: Dec 18th 2004

Police called to a brawl in a small town in Wales found themselves wrestling with 30 drunken Father Christmases. The fight broke out after 4,000 people in Santa costumes took part in a fun run in Newtown, Powys.
Issue 491: Dec 18th 2004

A shoplifter has been banned from every store in Wrexham after telling police she was just shopping the Romanian way. "It's okay to take things out of the store as long as you are going to go back and pay later," said Sandu Florenta, 18, who was caught with £65-worth of food, including three fresh chickens and four packs of frozen lamb, stuffed into a sack hidden up her skirt. "I do not understand British law. This would be okay in my country."
Issue 491: Dec 18th 2004

A man who stole a lorry in Vancouver was arrested after choking on the driver's spittle. The 26-year-old, who had nabbed the truck from outside a shopping centre, was bowling along the freeway when he mistook the driver's cup of tobacco-spit for a soft drink and took a swig. The thief started choking and had to stop and call 911 for help.
Issue 495: Jan 22nd 2005

The Costa Rican government is banning cheesy chat-up lines. Under the new law, men who use blatant flattery to get their way with the ladies could be fined or face up to 50 days in prison. "It will be hard for us to tell if the flattery is offensive or not," admitted a police spokesman in San José, "but we will trust the women's judgement."
Issue 498: Feb 12th 2005

Truck drivers who are caught speeding in India are being made to hop like frogs as a punishment. Police in Bihar have decided to humiliate drivers instead of taking them to court. Offenders have to sit on their haunches, hold their ears and hop for almost half a kilometre, while chanting the name of their favourite politician. "If they remember their leader when they are being punished, it's like they are insulting them," said a police spokesman. "If they have any sense, they won't [commit] the offence again."
Issue 499: Feb 19th 2005

A Turkish man has been arrested after disguising himself as his dead mother to collect her pension. Serafettin Gencel, 47, is said to have secretly buried his mother in his basement when she died two years ago. He then regularly donned her headscarf, stockings and overcoat to withdraw her pension from a bank in Balikesir, western Turkey. But the bank manager, suspicious of his deep voice, secretly photo-graphed Gencel and alerted the police.

Issue 503: March 19th 2005

A bogus policeman is being investigated in Austria for stopping female drivers for speeding. He claims it was the only way he could meet women. The man, who bought a uniform from a fancy dress shop and put a flashing light on his car, told a real police officer: "I was hoping one of them would fancy a man in uniform and give me their phone number, but it didn't work."

Issue 505: April 2nd 2005

An 82-year-old thief who used his mobility scooter as a getaway vehicle was spared jail this week. Widower George Brignall swiped a parcel of books from a doorstep in Goole, East Yorkshire, before fleeing the scene at 6mph, shaking off a witness who tried to apprehend him. He was arrested at his care home, fined £30 and ordered to pay £61.15 compensation.

Issue 507: April 16th 2005

A man on a stag night won a £20 bet by letting down a police car's tyres, only to discover there were two officers sitting inside. Jason Lee James, 34, was thrilled with his drunken stunt – until the officers arrested him for criminal damage. "They were sitting in the car when they heard a loud hissing noise," a court in Rhondda heard. "They found James crouching by the wheels letting the air out." He was fined £100.

Issue 507: April 16th 2005

Two boat thieves trying to escape the police rowed around in circles before being captured. The two men had broken into a Norwegian ship, but when an alarm went off they jumped into a dinghy that was tethered to the boat and grabbed an oar each. Unfortunately, neither had ever rowed before, so they each pulled in different directions. After watching the pair row round and round in circles for a while, the police arrested them.

Issue 510: May 7th 2005

A fleet of mourners looted a garage after stopping for petrol. Two hearses and four limos stopped at the Texaco garage in Fishguard, Pembrokeshire. While the cars were being filled up, 30 mourners ran inside and stripped the shelves of food and drink. "It happened so fast none of us could do anything" said manager Robert Bowen.
Issue 511: May 14th 2005

A Peeping Tom triggered a bomb scare in New York last week. A passer-by called the police after spotting a box full of wires poking through a subway grate. The street was sealed off and the bomb squad rushed to the scene – only to discover that the device was in fact a camera, positioned to take pictures up women's skirts. "It's disturbing," said one resident. "I'm happy I wear pants most of the time."
Issue 513: May 28th 2005

A Staffordshire youth has been threatened with an Asbo – even though he hasn't been born yet. Expectant mother Julie Brown received a letter from the council accusing her unborn child of annoying neighbours by playing outside on his motor scooter. "The letter is addressed to us personally," says Miss Brown, who is due to give birth in September. "I just hope it's not an omen that he's going to be naughty."
Issue 520: July 16th 2005

A man in Brazil has been arrested for stealing toothbrushes – even though he has no teeth. Ednor Rodrigues, 32, was caught on CCTV stealing seven toothbrushes from a supermarket in Ribeirao Preto. He initially denied everything, showing police officers his toothless mouth, but eventually confessed: "I don't know why I did it. I have no teeth, what was I thinking?"
Issue 524: August 6th 2005

A work of art consisting of a bottle of melted Antarctic ice has been stolen, and possibly drunk, by a thirsty thief at a literary festival in Devon. Valued at £42,000, and entitled Weapon of Mass Destruction, it was intended to highlight the dangers of global warming. "It looked like an ordinary bottle of water," said artist Wayne Hill, "but it was on a plinth and labelled."
Issue 525: August 20th 2005

A Russian man attempted to bribe a police officer and then destroy the evidence by eating all the money. The man, from Ussurisk in eastern Russia, had been arrested on minor drug charges when he sidled up to the investigating officer and offered him £1,200 to drop the case. When the officer refused, he began frantically stuffing the notes into his mouth. He only managed to swallow one before being charged with attempting to bribe a public official.
Issue 535: Oct 29th 2005

Two Chinese man have been arrested after trying to sneak across the Russian border on a lawnmower. When apprehended by border guards, they claimed they had got lost while cutting the grass.
Issue 537: Nov 12th 2006

A US prisoner who violated his parole was apprehended while trying to escape on a stolen lawnmower. Police in Illinois were able to track Charles H. Carter, 45, because he was wearing an ankle tag while under house arrest. They found him riding the lawnmower through the middle of a cornfield, which gave them plenty of time to set up a perimeter guard and ask him to stop. "He was only going four or five miles per hour," said Deputy Sheriff Jim Tapscott, "so I got out and jogged alongside him."
Issue 541: Dec 10th 2005

A German drink driver who tried to telephone a breakdown service was arrested after calling the police by mistake. Markus Fillbach, 31, tried to call a recovery service after one of his tyres burst in Monheim, Germany. "You'd better be quick because I'm pretty drunk and don't have a licence so it wouldn't be good if the cops drove past," he unwittingly told a police operator. Officers immediately raced to the scene, and arrested him for being seven times over the limit. "He wanted us to come quickly so we did," said a police spokesman.
Issue 542: Dec 17th 2005

A Memphis woman allegedly plotted to rob and kill four men after mistaking a block of cheese in their home for a giant brick of cocaine. Police claim that, after catching a glimpse of the white, crumbly queso fresco cheese, Jessica Sandy Booth asked a hit man to murder the men so she could snatch their stash. Her plot was foiled because the hit man turned out to be an undercover cop.
Issue 544: Jan 7th 2006

A Croatian armed robber fled empty-handed after a cashier slapped him around the face. The man, thought to be in his twenties, entered a betting shop in Zagreb and demanded the day's takings. Unfazed by his gun, Ana Zuric, 47, pulled off his mask, slapped him and said: "Don't be such a silly boy."
Issue 548: Feb 4th 2006

A German pensioner has confessed to a crime he committed 80 years ago. Helmut Bleibtreu, 84, from Herne, planted a firecracker on the track at his local railway station in 1926. Weighed down by guilt, he finally handed himself into police. The police told him that the case had passed the statute of limitations and that the offence had never been reported in the first place, but warned him not to do it again.
Issue 548: Feb 4th 2006

Better Off Behind Bars

A trampoline was installed at Chisbeck County Jail in Iowa, USA, after prisoners produced statistics proving that open-air trampolining had a beneficial effect on them. Six of them then propelled themselves over the prison fence; three remain at large. "They also asked for tunnel-digging equipment for a play they were doing about miners, said governor Clifton McPip, "but I refused. I'm not a fool."
Issue 89: Feb 15th 1997

A prisoner weighing 23 stone who tried to hang himself in a jail in Manila, the Philippines, brought down the roof. Five inmates escaped.
Issue 118: Sept 6th 1997

Two prisoners fleeing from jail in Gary, Texas, rang a radio station to announce their escape and won a £300 prize for the day's "best news item from a listener".
Issue 277: Oct 14th 2000

A 24-year-old Lithuanian woman has won the world's first prison beauty contest. The Miss Captivity contest was held in Lithuania's Panevezys Penal Labour Colony to determine the prettiest woman currently serving time. The winner, Samantha, fought back tears as she was presented with her crown. Asked by reporters what she'd like to do with her life, she replied: "I'd like to get out of prison right now."
Issue 385: Nov 23rd 2002

A Berlin factory owner has imposed prison-like conditions on his employees – and productivity has shot through the roof. Peter Hastlern has replaced his managers with prison guards, forces employees to address each other by an assigned number, and places workers in solitary confine-ment if they arrive late. Since the reforms were introduced, Hastlern Industries' profits and employee attendance has improved ten-fold. "We provide the discipline that most people crave, but lack in their private lives," says Hastlern.
Issue 386: Nov 30th 2002

Two murderers who planned to get married in Broadmoor called off their wedding after discovering just how evil the other one was. Sharon Carr and Robbie Layne, who are both serving life sentences, had already bought each other gold rings. But after they each read newspaper reports of their respective killings, the couple were horrified. They stormed out of the room and won't even talk to each other now.
Issue 395: Feb 8th 2003

A Florida man travelled to North Dakota to commit a robbery because he wanted to be jailed in Fargo – the safest prison in America. Alexander Strathas held up a motel and then turned himself into the police. He told authorities he was a habitual criminal, and if he was going to spend most of his life in prison, he wanted it to be a nice one.
Issue 397: Feb 22nd 2003

Moscow's governor has devised a new TV talent show in which prisoners will sing for their freedom. The show, called The Red Snowballberry, will feature hundreds of singing Russian convicts. The one with the best voice will be released from jail. But legal experts have expressed concern that the Russian mob may try to hack into the voting computers and manipulate the results in order to free their associates.
Issue 402: March 29th 2003

Fifteen prisoners escaped from a jail in Nigeria by weakening the walls with urine. "The walls are very weak," said a spokesman for the Kigo prison. "They must have urinated on the same spot repeatedly until they made a hole. They must have planned it for a very long time."
Issue 407: May 3rd 2003

A prisoner has confessed to three more crimes to add to his 184 convictions, because he wants to finish a catering course in prison. Gary Cowan, 35, even took police to the scenes of two robberies and a burglary so that they could collect evidence against him. Cambridge crown court last week sentenced him to an extra three years.
Issue 417: July 12th 2003

Two Turkish jailbirds who fell in love drilled a 3-inch hole through the prison wall that separated them, in order to procreate. The hole was only discovered when the mother – a convicted bomber – was found to be pregnant. She and the father – a murderer – were fined for damaging prison property.
Issue 502: March 12th 2005

An armed robber has welcomed a nine-year jail sentence, saying it will aid his studies into the criminal mind. John L. Stanley, 61, was caught wearing a fake moustache and counting his loot after robbing a bank in Kansas. He told the judge that he had botched things deliberately, because he was studying criminology and needed first-hand experience of jail. "You can take a butterfly and put it on a light stand," he explained, "but until you are a butterfly and fly, you can't understand why a butterfly flies."
Issue 508: April 23rd 2005

An Arizona sheriff ordered 700 convicts to walk to jail clad only in pink shorts and flip-flops. The convicts, who were being transferred to a new jail, had to walk for two miles through the streets of Phoenix, linked by pink handcuffs. Sheriff Joe Arpaio said the humiliation would do them good. "They can see this is what happens to people who break the law."
Issue 509: April 30th 2005

A Romanian thief is suing the state for failing to cure him of his criminal ways. Danut Mester, 38, spent 13 years in prison for theft. The week he got out he stole again, and was slapped back into jail. Now he is suing the state for £200,000, claiming: "I am just a victim of the system. I committed antisocial crimes after I was released because the authorities never helped reintegrate me into society."
Issue 509: April 30th 2005

A mother-of-three has chosen to go to prison rather than pay a parking fine, so she can take a break from her chores. Maria Brunner, from Poing in Germany, waved happily to neighbours as police drove her away after she refused to settle the £2,500 fine. "As long as I get food and a hot shower every day, I don't mind," she said. "It means I can finally get some rest and relaxation."
Issue 511: May 14th 2005

Sexy Beasts

A Brazilian from Recife is being sued for refusing to pay for a mechanical penis transplant because it operates every time neighbours use their TV remote control.
Issue 14: August 26th 1995

Would-be model Britt Royle has argued that her newly enlarged breasts will give her a business edge and so should be tax deductable. "Our inspector will look closely at the case," said a Revenue official.
Issue 15: 2nd Sept 1995

Two grandmothers, both aged 78, have been arrested for prostitution in Taiwan. They explained to the police that they could not resist their sexual urges.
Issue 31: Dec 23rd 1995

Italian stripper Carlo Pampini, 31, was performing in a Naples hotel when disaster struck. "I knew from the outset they were going to be a hard audience. They were older than usual, and very serious". Unfazed, he removed his clothes and wedged a large sausage between his buttocks, urging one woman to remove it with her teeth. At this point the audience set upon him and beat him senseless with their chairs. It later emerged that what he had taken for a hen party was a meeting of the Catholic Mothers Against Pornography Guild.
Issue 100: July 12th 1997

Stripper Busty Heart is being sued for £200,000 after hitting a man around the head with her 88 inch bosoms. He claimed he was hurt by her breasts, which weigh 3 stone each, during a party trick at an Illinois club.
Issue 112: July 29th 1997

27 year-old Debbie Wolf, from Cambridge, suffers from a rare condition known as Sliders phenomenon, which means she gives off a huge static charge when aroused. Debbie, who was sacked from a nightclub for blowing the sound system, breaks 30 lightbulbs a week during sex with her husband Oliver, and has also affected the street lamps outside her home.
Issue 113: August 2nd 1997

A British Columbian woman is suing a chemist for $500,000, after she bought a popular contraceptive jelly, ate it on toast, and became pregnant. The product was labelled "jelly" and kept just two aisles from the food section. "Who has time to sit around reading directions these days," she said, "especially when you're sexually aroused?"
Issue 116: August 23rd 1997

A church congregation was stunned when the sound system picked up two lovers on a mobile phone arranging to meet for sex. The couple were the local deputy sheriff in Nashville, Tennessee, and the vicar's wife.
Issue 154: May 23rd 1998

Japanese salesmen are being forced to take part in sex and drinking contests to prove they are worthy of promotion – all because firms think that men who are good in bed are good at business. One Tokyo boss sent four would-be managers to a brothel every night for a month. The prostitutes were paid to keep a record of their boozing and rate their performances. "The more we drank and the longer we performed the better the marks," said Tadayoshi Ito, 28. "The winner downed 15 beers and then had sex with 3 girls till 5am. It sounds like paradise but it was torture, drinking and whoring night after night."
Issue 155: May 30th 1998

Gerhard Kittel, 93, has given 150 pre-World War II condoms to a museum in Furth, Germany. He said he didn't need them any more.
Issue 170: Sept 12th 1998

Petrol stations in western China are luring motorists to the pumps with a free gift – a session with a prostitute once they have filled up with fuel.
Issue 172: Sept 26th 1988

A clergyman was forced to do a striptease on stage after a mob of drunken women mistook him for a strip-o-gram. The Reverend Tim Peeps was driving past the Flagne Bar in Sydney, Australia, when his car broke down. He went in to ask for help, but was seized by 30 female revellers who had ordered a priest-o-gram. "When I protested... they threatened to castrate me," he recalled. It wasn't until the real stripper arrived that they returned his clothes and gave his car a push.
Issue 185: Jan 2nd 1999

When The Sun asked its readers whether they would sleep with Robin Cook, 966 rang to say they would. But 7,303 callers vetoed "nookie with Cookie". The Sun "was amazed anyone admitted fancying the minister".
Issue 187: Jan 16th 1999

A court witness who was asked if she was sexually active during a trial in Dallas, Texas, replied: "No, I just lie there."
Issue 191: Feb 13th 1999

Amorous couple Mick Pallant and Danielle Minns were discovered by a security guard whilst entwined in a Sainsbury's refrigerated unit. The couple fled, covered in cream and yoghurt, but were later arrested and fined £40. "Funny thing is," said Pallant, "we'd done the same thing the week before at Budgens and they were fine about it."
Issue 201: April 24th 1999

Odd job man Antonio Lobo is taking a blonde aristocrat to court for fobbing him off with sex every time he asked her to pay her bills, reports the News of the World. Lobo claims Anita Forsyth-Forrest from Wiltshire owes him around £16,000. "Sex with Anita was the best I've ever had," he said. "But she seems to think it paid for all her house repairs. I can't live off orgasms."
Issue 204: May 15th 1999

Brazil's most popular children's TV presenter, Tizinha (Little Auntie), has fallen foul of the country's church leaders. Tizinha appears on her quiz show in S&M outfits and whips contestants who answer questions incorrectly. The dominatrix was accused of being a "disgusting mole" by one religious organisation. "I wet on the boots of bigots and I whip their ears with a fly swat," she responded.
Issue 215: July 31st 1999

A sex pest in Austria has been arrested for making over 40,000 calls to Viennese women. He was caught after a woman he had rung every day for six months said: "I'm too busy to talk to you now but give me your number and I'll call you back."
Issue 215: July 31st 1999

A taxi driver in Sweden who left the meter running while making love to a female passenger in the back seat has been found guilty of overcharging. The court ruled that the cabbie had exploited the woman's need for sex during 25 different journeys over the course of two months.
Issue 224: Oct 2nd 1999

Accountant Luis Camargo, 43, from Bogota, Colombia, disguised himself as an alien in order to fool suburban women into having sex with him. "He was so cute," 23-year-old secretary Andrea Durano told investigating officers. "He was all green and I was so excited to be with a real space alien." He told the women that he was an observer from the planet Zonda and that if they pleased him he would take them on trips to outer space.
Issue 239: Jan 22nd 2000

Italian waiter Marcus Fedel, 24, was cleared of indecently assaulting a tourist after he told a Milan court: "I pinched her bottom. She said it made her feel young. So I pinched her again."
Issue 267: August 5th 2000

The owner of a York sex shop faces court action because his films are not sexy enough. Nick Griffin is being prosecuted after a number of customers complained that his £35 "hardcore" films were not nearly as raunchy as he claimed.
Issue 271: Sept 2nd 2000

Patrick Lawrence, 22, was arrested in Washington for attempting to make love to a pumpkin. Asked by police why he was molesting a pumpkin, he replied: "Pumpkin? Damn, is it midnight already?"
Issue 274: Sep 23rd 2000

The madam of a legal brothel in Sydney, Australia, has complained to the local council about plans to build a church nearby. She says it will attract the wrong sort of people to the area.
Issue 279: Oct 28th 2000

A 20-year-old woman in Taiwan has had a mobile phone surgically removed from her bottom. She told doctors that the Nokia 8850 got stuck when a sex game went wrong.
Issue 295: Feb 24th 2001

The Sun last week unveiled its latest scoop – the first soldier ever to go topless on Page 3. Lance Corporal Roberta Winterton, a PT instructor who trains squaddies in Chippenham, Wilts, risked the wrath of the Army's top brass by running off to London to try her hand at glamour modelling. "The Army is not for me," she told the paper. "I want to do topless but it has got to be tasteful and classy like it is in The Sun."
Issue 294: Feb 17th 2001

A sex researcher in Italy has invented a pair of "chastity knickers" which call husbands' mobiles when their wives take off their pants. The £44 undies have a built-in sensor which phones suspicious partners if the pants go down for more than five minutes. Dr Giuseppe Cirillo, who developed the knickers, claims they are selling out.
Issue 300: March 31st 2001

A council in Brazil has voted to organise an annual Orgasm Day. The 35,000 inhabitants of Esperantina will be urged to work harder to achieve sexual satisfaction on 9 May. Councillor Arimateia Dantas had the idea after losing a girlfriend because of his premature ejaculation problem. He explained: "My ex-partner was very hot, but she took such a time to reach orgasm that I could not wait."
Issue 336: Dec 8th 2001

A female employee of a New Zealand sawmill was out after work with two male managers when one said: "Jesus, you don't scrub up too bad, do you?" He then fell to his knees and bit her bottom. She lost her case for harassment because the incident happened after work.
Issue 343: Feb 2nd 2002

A Humberside chef has been found guilty of having sex with a goat in an allotment. Stephen Hall was arrested after a train stopped at signals and dozens of horrified passengers spotted him mid-coitus and rang 999. Two passers-by wrestled Hall to the ground while officers raced to the scene. Detective Crinnion told the court: "I saw the goat the next day. It did not seem upset, but it is difficult to tell."
Issue 344: Feb 9th

Canadian police are hunting a woman in her forties who burst into a petrol station with a knife and fondled the 17-year-old male cashier before performing oral sex on him. According to the owners of the Toronto petrol station, the incident has prompted a flood of job applications from teenage boys.
Issue 351: March 30th 2002

The Naked Truth, a Bulgarian news show in which female newsreaders disrobe while presenting the news, has been banned after it trounced the state-broadcast news in the ratings.
Issue 357: May 11th 2002

An Australian brothel has closed down after American sailors exhausted its prostitutes. The Langtrees brothel in Perth took 580 bookings in three days when three US warships docked in the harbour last month. Owner Mary-Anne Kenworthy said she had now closed her doors because the girls were too worn out to perform to their usual high standards. "I would not sell a man a hamburger if I thought my buns were stale."
Issue 357: May 11th 2002

Taiwanese police are trying to coax the island's oldest prostitute into retirement. Grandma Chiu, 82, says she needs to work to supplement her pension. But younger prostitutes have complained that she is undercutting them, charging one-tenth of their rates. Police have embarked on a fundraising campaign to pay her off, and have asked social workers to find her somewhere cheaper to live. "She actually looks surprisingly good for her age," said one officer. "With a little make-up, she can pass for a 70-year-old."
Issue 359: May 25th 2002

Los Angeles school teacher Tracy Niederkirk has been fired after stripping naked in an anatomy class. She claimed she was merely pointing out the finer details of the female body.
Issue 364: June 29th 2002

One in 200 women becomes sexually aroused when frisked with a metal-detecting wand, according to a new US study. "These women will often act in a suspicious manner to provoke airport security guards into using wands," says the report.
Issue 370: August 10th 2002

A Swedish politician has called for more sex on TV to help boost the country's birth rate. "I want more porn on TV," said Christian Democrat Teres Kirpikli. "For example, every Saturday, all day. That will give people the lust to have sex. There's nothing wrong with watching porn. I have done it with my husband many times, and it was good."
Issue 375: Sept 14th 2002

An Italian judge has ruled that men have the right to slap the bottoms of female co-workers. According to the ruling by Italy's highest court, patting a woman's bottom does not constitute sexual harassment if it's a one-time gesture carried out on the spur of the moment "and in the spirit of fun".
Issue 389: Dec 21st 2002

The Thai health ministry has launched an exercise program to help women increase their bust size. Health officials say that the exercises will help cheer up women who feel depressed by media images of big-breasted Western women. "Regularly taking bosom firming classes can make their wishes come true," said a spokesman.
Issue 397: Feb 22nd 2003

Romanian prostitutes are diversifying their trade. Hit by recession, they are now offering to do household chores for their clients after sex. The women will vacuum, cook meals and scrub floors. "The girls help these men get rid of the three things which torment their lives: sex, cleaning and cooking," says one pimp.
Issue 398: March 1st 2003

Millions of cable TV viewers in Washington were treated to ten hours of free hardcore porn after computers went haywire. But the cable operator only received 11 complaints – from people worried that they might have to pay for the service.
Issue 414: June 14th 2003

An Italian woman has been banned from screaming during night-time sex sessions, because she is keeping her neighbours awake.
Her husband told a court in Treviso: "I can't do it unless she screams. Otherwise it's like having sex with a cushion." But the judge warned the woman she faces jail unless she keeps it down, so the newlyweds now have sex at lunchtime.
Issue 417: July 12th 2003

Lost property staff at a pub chain have collected 124 discarded bras. Brannigans has now set up a telephone hotline to reunite women with their underwear. "It seems some of our customers cannot wait to get out of their undies," said a spokesman.
Issue 421: August 9th 2003

A disabled Dutchman who was awarded a £100-a-month state sex allowance has encountered an unexpected difficulty: he can't find a prostitute willing to give him the receipt required by his local council. The prostitutes say they are afraid of being caught by the taxman.
Issue 423: August 23rd 2003

A woman who has up to 288 orgasms a day is seeking medical help, because she says too much pleasure is a pain. Jean Lund, 51, from LA, suffers from a rare condition called permanent sexual arousal syndrome, which she developed after undergoing surgery on a shoulder nerve. Cycling and horse-riding are out of bounds, and she hasn't dared to make love for seven years. "My worst nightmare is public transport," says Mrs Lund. "The vibrations on buses makes things so much worse."
Issue 437: Nov 29th 2003

Residents of F*cking, in Austria, have rejected plans to change the name of their village. The population of 150 had considered a new name to stop their road signs being stolen by tourists. "Everyone here knows what it means in English," says mayor Siegfried Hoeppel, "but for us F*cking is F*cking – and it's going to stay F*cking."
Issue 465: June 19th 2004

Police in Quebec have warned motorists not to have sex while driving. The announcement followed a fatal car crash involving an amorous couple. "They were having sexual intercourse at the wheel of the vehicle," said a police spokesman. "This makes driving that much more dangerous."
Issue 481: Oct 9th 2004

A new reality TV show has been launched in Germany to find the man with the fastest sperm. The sperm will be attracted to the finishing line by a chemical lure identical to that emitted by the female egg in the womb. Doctors will judge the winner, and the owner of the sperm will be crowned Germany's most virile man.
Issue 496: Jan 29th 2005

A strip club in Boise, Idaho, has found a way round indecency laws: patrons are given pencils and paper when they go in, and the club is advertised as a life-drawing class. Public nudity is forbidden in Boise "unless it has serious artistic merit". The Erotic City's "Art Night" has been a hit, says owner Chris Teague. "We have a lot of people drawing some very good pictures."
Issue 501: March 5th

A couple in Devon who set out in a dinghy for an amorous voyage were interrupted when their cries of passion were mistaken for cries for help. A man walking his dog along the cliff called 999 after spotting the dinghy "rocking vigorously". Two lifeboats were launched and raced to the scene, only to find the couple in flagrante. The dinghy was escorted back to the beach where the embarrassed pair were reprimanded by waiting police officers. "I've never seen such things in a six-foot inflatable at such an early hour," said lifeboatman Nigel Crang.
Issue 523: August 6th 2005

A Chinese company is marketing condoms named after Bill Clinton and Monica Lewinsky. Liu Wenhua, a spokesman for the Guangzhou Rubber Group, said the names were not chosen for satirical or comic effect, but because the former president is viewed in China as the sort of "responsible and dedicated" man who would always practise safe sex. "The Clinton condom will be the top of our line," says Liu. "The Lewinsky condom is not quite as good."
Issue 532: Oct 8th 2005

An analyst for BT Futurology has designed a pair of musical breast implants. The recipient would have an MP3 player implanted in one breast, and their music collection in the other. The sound would be transmitted wirelessly to headphones, with volume, and so on, controlled by a bluetooth panel worn on the wrist. "If a woman has something implanted permanently, it might as well do something useful," said Ian Pearson.
Issue 534: Oct 22nd 2005

A doctor in New Zealand has closed his surgery and turned it into a brothel. His patients are furious, but Dr Neil Benson thinks it's a logical move. "It's about providing a private service and maintaining confidentiality, which is what my medical practice was about, so it's not a big leap."
Issue 548: Feb 4th 2006

God On Our Side

In Thailand, a rainmaker died after a rocket he had launched to appease the gods fell to earth and landed on his head.
Issue 109: July 5th 1997

Mexican priest and former pilot Armando Capaldi, 43, decided to use his flying skills to pretend he was God and spread the Word. Donning white robes and a false beard, he set off over the suburbs of Mexico City in a hired motorglider, bellowing: "I am come to thee, oh my people!" through a Tannoy. Alas, in his enthusiasm he flew too low, caught his foot on a cable and lost control of the glider, which plummeted to Earth in the middle of a large fruit market, injuring four people.
Issue 148: April 11th 1998

A sign outside an Idaho church reads: "If you're done with sin, c'mon in." Underneath it, someone has written in lipstick: "And if you're not, call Rita on..."
Issue 157: June 13th 1998

Pope John Paul II, 78, plans to end rumours of ill health by making a 120 ft bungee-jump. "He thinks this will be the perfect way to attract more young people to the church," says a Vatican source. The Pope's plunge is pencilled in for 31 March.
Issue 193: Feb 27th 1999

Priest Andreas Pendel, 40, has been defrocked after offering 30 women sex in exchange for absolution of their sins in Bucharest, Romania. Most accepted.
Issue 224: Oct 2nd 1999

A tribe of Brazilian headhunters has apologised for the killing of a Catholic missionary called Father Robert in 1925. The tribe sent a remorseful letter to the Vatican, accompanied by the victim's shrunken head.
Issue 251: April 15th 2000

Ravindara Kadadi, an 88-year-old Swami from Bombay, has been charged with endangering public health after levitating two baby elephants. "When the elephants went up they got excited and manure began to rain down," said witness Kumar Bhatta. "I was hit by some small lumps but my wife really got it." After enduring the swami's act, 13 people have filed charges.
Issue 269: August 19th 2000

A woman who stopped at traffic lights in Detroit noticed a bumper sticker on the car in front reading: "Honk if you love Jesus". When she did exactly that, the driver suffered an attack of road rage, got out and bashed a dent in her bonnet with a baseball bat.
Issue 279: Oct 28th 2000

A German billionaire is waging a one-man crusade to rid the world of demons. "In recent years, armies of demons have been seen wreaking destruction everywhere," said industrialist Ernst Grueber. "I want to use my God-given wealth to help rid the world of evil." To this end, Grueber is offering $1 million to anyone who catches a demon and delivers it dead or alive to his mansion.
Issue 281: Nov 11th 2000

A request in the Churchdown Parish Magazine reads: "Would the congregation please note that the bowl at the back of the church, labelled "For The Sick" is for monetary donations only."
Issue 299: March 24th 2001

Graham Eldridge, 14, was struck by lightning in Luton, while writing a religious education essay on why he did not believe in heaven. He escaped with slight burns.
Issue 307: May 19th 2001

A pious dog living in Texas wakes up at 5am every morning to make the lonely trek from its master's farmhouse to a Catholic church 15 miles away, and back again. Members of the congregation say Sacha seems especially devoted to St Peter and "rapturously stares" at his statue during mass. Sacha's owner, farmer Anton Diaz, claims he never encouraged the dog to go to church. "One morning she just left the sheep and walked to chapel," he says.
Issue 320: August 18th 2001

A Pittsburgh woman died after imagining she saw Jesus by the roadside, surrounded by angels ascending to heaven. Filled with religious rapture, she hurled herself out of the sun-roof of her husband's car. What she had actually seen was Ernie Jenkins on his way to a party dressed as Jesus. He had stopped by the side of the road when his disciples – 12 helium-filled sex dolls – came loose from their moorings in his truck and started to drift off.
Issue 322: Sept 21st 2001

A woman in Utah has won nearly £200,000 in damages from a fundamentalist church which failed to deliver on its promise that she would meet Jesus. Kaziah Hancock gave 67 acres of her farm to the True and Living Church of Jesus Christ of Saints of the Last Days. In return church founder, Jim Harmston, said she would meet Jesus in the flesh. When the Messiah failed to show, she sued for breach of contract.
Issue 344: Feb 9th 2002

America's largest Baptist group is urging members to boycott Howard Johnson hotels after the chain agreed to host an S&M festival in Missouri entitled "Beat Me in St Louis" – a follow-up to the successful "Spanksgiving" held last November.
Issue 354: April 20th 2002

Mourners at an Alabama funeral attacked a preacher who made insulting remarks about the deceased. In a brutally honest eulogy, Rev Orlando Bethel branded the late Lish Taylor a "drunkard and a fornicator" who was "burning in hell". When his microphone was switched off, the preacher produced a megaphone and called the bereaved "whoremongers", after which they attacked him, dragging him down the aisle.
Issue 365: July 6th 2002

An American man has died and left his fortune to the son of God. Ernest Digweed, of Palm Springs, left his entire estate to Jesus Christ Our Saviour, guaranteeing Jesus an annual income of $615,820 for the next 30 years. Digweed's heirs are contesting the will, and have offered to take out an insurance policy for the full inheritance, payable to the Messiah upon his return.
Issue 379: Oct 12th 2002

A French priest who was pulled over for speeding has claimed "the devil made me do it". Father Laguerie was on his way to Paris to deliver a lecture on the topic of sin when he said his car inexplicably picked up speed – to 120mph. "I can only assume some evil force took over," he told police.
Issue 396: Feb 15th 2003

A penitent Italian man really went to town at confession. After pouring his heart out to the priest at the Bozzola Sanctuary, the man handed over a bag containing two guns, two hand grenades and 18 bullets. "I couldn't believe my eyes," said Father Gregorio Vitale. "I cannot say what the man confessed to. I am just happy that he wanted to return to the Church."
Issue 403: April 5th 2003

A Bible theme park is being planned for the site of the Garden of Eden in Iraq. American investors are planning to build a Disney-style theme park, complete with roller coasters and other thrill rides, on the religious site 85 miles south west of Al Kut. Actors wearing only fig leaves will reconstruct the daily lives of Adam and Eve. Robert Herskins, who is to design the theme park, thinks it's a "terrific idea. As a tourist attraction, it could be the jewel of the New Iraq".
Issue 416: July 5th 2003

A Birmingham, Alabama, preacher has left the Church because he thinks God played a terrible practical joke on him. Reverend Paul Taler was walking past a construction site when he suddenly started ascending towards heaven. "I'm going home in the rapture!" he shouted. Actually, a crane had snagged his clothing. "It was a real nasty trick the Lord played on me," says Taler. "What's next? A whoopee cushion?"
Issue 418: July 19th 2003

A vicar handed out hardcore porn to his parishioners after a mix-up at a video factory. Almost 300 churchgoers in Lampoldshausen, Germany received an X-rated film instead of Rev Frithjof's Christmas video. But the vicar is looking on the bright side. "The project has received enormous publicity through the mix-up," he says, "and best of all, the people who ordered the porn now have our films about Jesus."
Issue 439: Dec 13th 2003

An American Christian group is lobbying to have the whale reclassified as a fish, because that is how the animal is described in the story of Jonah. "The Bible is God's own words," says a spokesman for Concerned Christians for Education Reform. "If the Lord says the whale is a 'great fish', it's a fish. Period."
Issue 462: May 29th 2004

Teachers at a fundamentalist Christian school in Norway have complained that the headmaster keeps trying to perform exorcisms on them. Three teachers at the Skjaergard school – previously criticised for listing Jesus Christ as its executive manager – claim that Pastor Glenn Rasmussen tried to free them from "evil spirits" during working hours. "He grabbed my stomach and started yelling loudly," says Borre Olsen. "I didn't feel possessed by evil spirits, but there are no limits to what you are going to experience in life."
Issue 474: August 21st 2004

A Romanian priest has been ordered to live in seclusion on just bread and water for a month, as a punishment for delivering a five-hour sermon at a funeral. Agapie Aurel Rusu was reportedly seeking revenge on the relatives of the dead man, who had wanted another priest to take the service. Father Rusul's oration covered topics as diverse as politics, history and heart surgery, with quotations from epic poems to illustrate his points.
Issue 476: Sept 4th 2004

Religious leaders are up in arms over claims that magician David Blaine plans to part the Red Sea on live television. "Mr Blaine should play his little tricks on the concrete walkways of Brooklyn," says Calvary Church leader Timothy Muirson. "How dare he set foot onto that holy place?" Blaine has not confirmed the rumour, but TV networks are already jostling for the broadcasting rights.
Issue 485: Nov 6th 2004

An Australian vicar is to launch the world's first all-nude church services. Robert Wright, who has been a naturist for 16 years, says like-minded Christians need a place where they can worship starkers. He plans to hold weekly services at a nudist resort near Brisbane. "Nude is not rude," he says. "We are not into sex orgies, we are very well-adjusted people."
Issue 504: March 26th 2005

Villagers in Croatia have rallied in support of their local priest, after he was suspended for running up a £16,000 bill on a telephone sex line. Father Ljubomir Simunovic – whose parishioners are refusing to go to church until he is reinstated – spent hours on the phone to a sex line operator, but insists he was just giving her spiritual guidance. "I had no idea she was working on a sex hotline, I didn't even know such a thing existed," he says. "I thought I was helping a woman who had returned to God after her divorce while struggling to support a son on her own."
Issue 510: May 7th 2005

Buddhist monks from rival temples have been arrested for brawling. The monks were collecting alms on opposite sides of the street in Nong Khai, Thailand, when one group gave the other "the finger". The ensuing fight had to be broken up by police. The monks were later defrocked – but one was unrepentant. "If senators can fight in parliament, why can't monks?" asked Boonlert Boonpan.
Issue 515: June 11th 2005

A Belgian nun has been reprimanded by her mother superior for "indecorous" dancing at Catholic World Youth Day held in Germany this August. Sister Johanne Vertommen, 29, was photographed with her legs wrapped around a missionary as he held her up in the air. "At such occasions I get carried away by the enthusiasm of the group," she explained.
Issue 527: Sept 3rd 2005

One of Thailand's top monks has recorded a series of Buddhist sayings as phone ringtones. Phra Phayom Kalayano says his ringtones will help steer young minds away from "unwholesome thoughts". They include phrases such as: "Compose yourself before answering this call. Avoid being irascible and causing disputes"; and "It is better to sweat from hard work than cry from laziness, which encourages poverty".
Issue 530: Sept 24th 2005

A convicted murderer in Romania is trying to sue God for failing to protect him from the Devil. The prisoner, known only as Pavel M, claims that his baptism was a contract between him and the Almighty, and that the Almighty – in the form of the Romanian Orthodox Church – broke its terms by allowing temptation to lead him off the path of righteousness.
Issue 534: Oct 22nd 2005

Accidents Will Happen

A university student in Liverpool who injured his leg in an effort to escape "giant mice" is suing the hypnotist who induced the hallucination. They were only small mice, the hypnotist said in his defence.
Issue 9: July 22nd 1995

A man crossing a road holding a banner saying "The end of the world is nigh" was hit by a lorry and killed in Madrid.
Issue 47: April 20th 1996

Tokyo jelly enthusiast Oso Kantaki died while attempting to create the world's largest jelly. He constructed a 20ft-high Perspex mould in his garden and poured fast-setting jelly solution into it. Mr Kantaki slipped into it and drowned. His wife found him suspended head first in solid jelly.
Issue 76: Nov 9th 1996

A hospital in Pelonomi, South Africa, found out why patients kept dying on Fridays when it was discovered that a cleaner was unplugging life-support machines to plug in the vacuum cleaner.
Issue 78: Nov 23rd 1996

Juan Versa, who survived four train crashes in two months, died after getting an electric shock as he played with his son's toy train set in Mexico City.
Issue 79: Nov 30th 1996

Eight people were injured when a 10-foot plastic sausage which was being hoisted onto the roof of a restaurant in a French skiing resort slipped out of its harness and onto the slope. Workman Rene Flatulle tried to control it by jumping on top but it took off downhill with him desperately clinging on. The sausage whizzed past skiers for almost quarter of a mile before crashing into a group of Nigerian civil servants, eight of whom were seriously hurt.
Issue 103: May 24th 1997

Retail trainee Animbo Anabayo, 23, lay dead in the window of a Johannesburg furniture store for a week before anyone noticed. He had collapsed while rearranging the water bed display. Passers-by assumed he was demonstrating how comfortable the beds were. Indeed, Anabayo looked so comfortable that waterbed sales quadrupled during the seven days he lay in the shop's window.
Issue 108: June 28th 1997

A helicopter was carrying 30 lavatories across Mexico City when the net holding them snapped. Twenty-nine of the ceramic bowls fell to the ground without harming a soul, but one plummeted through a roof and landed fatally on Fernando Huja, a systems analyst, who was sitting on his own lavatory at the time. "He was my second husband," said his distraught widow. "My first was crushed to death under a harpsichord."
Issue 116: August 23rd 1997

A Frenchman who believed he was the reincarnation of St Francis of Assisi, the patron saint of animals, was eaten alive when he tried to preach to lions in Nairobi, Kenya.
Issue 118: Sept 6th 1997

Kentucky resident Philip Johnson shot himself in the shoulder two years ago "to see what it felt like to be shot". When Johnson was taken to hospital again recently, a friend explained that the first shooting had "felt so good he had to do it again".
Issue 139: Feb 7th 1998

Nak-Hun Choe, 48, came second in a South Korean karaoke contest with Celine Dion's My Heart Will Go On, then died from a heart attack as he was given his prize.
Issue 154: May 23rd 1998

A man who had a heart attack halfway through a flight was saved by 40 heart specialists heading home from a conference. When Klaus Schmidt, 64, slumped in his seat, the chief steward asked: "Is there a doctor on board?" Forty hands shot up; the entire German delegation returning from a meeting in Dublin.
Issue 152: May 9th 1998

Surgeons were stunned to find a mobile phone jammed up a man's bottom. The patient told doctors in Rio, Brazil, that he had skidded in the shower and landed on his mobile phone which he had left on the bathroom floor. As hospital staff tried to get it out, it rang three times before stopping. "We wondered if he had an answering machine up there as well," said one of the doctors.
Issue 176: Oct 24th 1998

Dance teacher Alberto Fergo tangoed across the floor and straight out of a fifth floor window, falling 60ft to his death. Alberto had been telling his pupils in Lisbon, Portugal, that in order to keep the head held high they should focus on the ceiling.
Issue 179: Nov 14th 1998

John Boyman choked to death when he chewed the tassels off a stripper in a nightclub in Pennsylvania. John, 29, jumped on stage when exotic dancer Cherri Blossom stripped down to a pair of fluffy strings covering her breasts. He pulled one of the tassels off her nipple with his teeth, swallowed it and choked.
Issue 183: Dec 12th 1998

Flemming Petersen, from Frederikssund, Denmark, has been fined £200 for "mistreating" his father's corpse. He smuggled his father out of a morgue, dressed him in leathers and took him for a spin on his motorbike. Then he took him to a bar, propped him up, put a cigar in his mouth and chatted to him for an hour. After being fined, Petersen, said: "Everybody should be treated in a nice way."
Issue 188: Jan 23rd 1999

Personalised coffins are the latest fad in the US. Golfers can buy a Fairway to Heaven casket, made to look like a golf course, while Elvis fans can have theirs wrapped like a brown paper parcel and marked: "Return to Sender."
Issue 197: March 27th 1999

In Amsterdam a 99-year-old-heart patient leapt from his third-floor window rather than eat his hospital food. The patient survived after crashing through a tiled roof below, and doctors carried him back to bed for a restorative jam roly-poly.
Issue 199: April 10th 1999

When Cachi the poodle fell from a 13-storey block of flats in Buenos Aires, he caused a domino death effect. Marta Espina, 75, died instantly when the poodle landed on her head. Seconds later, Edith Sola, 46, who had stopped to watch the accident, was knocked down by a bus. This was too much for an unidentified old man who collapsed at Sola's feet with a heart attack. "I've never seen anything like it," said a detective. "There were bodies all over the place."
Issue 199: April 10th 1999

Two unlucky armed robbers in Alabama chose to hold up a local bar on the night it had been hired by the local gun club. Both died in a hail of bullets.
Issue 208: June 12th 1999

Belgian trucker Luc Duchateau died after wolfing down a bag of nails and a drill bit. His doctor had told him that increasing his iron intake would improve his sex drive. "I was talking about spinach, liver or dietary supplements," said the unnamed physician. "How was I to know the fool would order his meal from a hardware store?"
Issue 213: July 17th 1999

Hospitals near Greenwich have admitted eight patients showing signs of millennial psychosis. One claimed to have swallowed a millennium bug.
Issue 214: July 24th 1999

When Narsh Savita, from Kanpur, India, was dumped by his girlfriend, he decided to end it all. First, the 24 year-old hanged himself from a light fitting, only for the ceiling to collapse. Next, he tried to shoot himself, but ended up in prison after the bullet missed him and lodged in a neighbour's wall. Later, he decided to leap under the wheels of a train, only to be snatched back from the edge of the platform by commuters. For his 21st and final suicide bid, he hurled himself off the roof of a five-storey building – and landed in the back of a laundry truck.
Issue 221: Sept 11th 1999

A Thai circus troupe went into mourning after its trampolining dwarf accidentally bounced into the mouth of a yawning hippopotamus. The dwarf was swallowed by Hilda the hippo, who was waiting in the wings ready to appear in the following act. In Hilda's defence, vets explained that her swallowing mechanism was automatic and that she had never before eaten a fellow artiste.
Issue 228: Oct 30th 1999

In Lhasa, Tibet, over 8,000 women have asked the government for child support, claiming to have been impregnated by yetis. One woman explained: "A year ago, while sleeping, I was roughly grabbed by the back of my pyjama bottoms and carried to his foul-smelling cave, where he proceeded to have sex with me. It was not unpleasant. But I don't want my son teased by other children, saying 'Your Dad's a Yeti,' and refusing to play ball games with him." The Chinese authorities insist that the children, who are covered in fine white hairs, are merely the result of inbreeding in remote parts of the Himalayas.
Issue 233: Dec 4th 1999

A Chilean man has given up trying to vote after election officials repeatedly turned him away on the grounds that he was dead. Ernesto Alvear, 74, was told that he had been officially dead for ten years. "I'm tired of complaining," said Alvear. "I think this is the last time I'm going to bother."
Issue 236: Dec 25th 1999

An Indian farmer killed a policeman by breathing rancid curry fumes on him, reports The Star. While attempting to arrest Raji Bhattachara in Bhopal, India, the officer got a whiff of the herdsman's putrid breath and suffered a fatal asthma attack. Bhattachara, who lives on a spicy vegetarian diet and has never cleaned his teeth, is being charged with manslaughter.
Issue 245: March 4th 2000

Iraqi terrorist Khay Rahnajet sent a letter bomb with insufficient postage. When it came back with 'Return to Sender' stamped on the front, he absent-mindedly opened it and was blown to bits.
Issue 288: Dec 30th 2000

A proofreader at a New York publishing firm died at his desk in an open-plan office and remained there for five days before anyone noticed. George Turklebaum, 51, who had worked for the firm for 30 years, had a coronary on Monday, and was found dead by the cleaner on Saturday. "He was always absorbed in his work, the first in and the last to leave," said a colleague, "so no one noticed anything unusual."
Issue 290: Jan 20th 2001

A psychology student in New York rented out her spare room to a carpenter in order to study his reactions when she nagged him incessantly. After weeks of needling, he snapped and beat her up with an axe.
Issue 300: March 31st 2001

In the past three years, three Malaysian executioners have died while fooling around on the gallows. The last to go was posing for photographs with his head in the noose when the trap doors gave way under his weight. He was killed instantly.

Issue 306: May 12th 2001

Wracked with pain after accidentally cutting off his hand with a saw, 25-year-old William Barton tried to render himself unconscious by shooting himself a dozen times in the head with a nail gun. The Bethlehem construction worker survived the barrage of one-inch nails and his hand was later reattached in hospital.

Issue 316: July 21st 2001

A boy aged three threw a tantrum in a New Zealand chemist's shop and attacked two women shoppers. He kicked and punched them and hit them so hard with his toy truck that both needed hospital treatment, one for a fractured skull. His mother said: "Yeah, he does that sometimes."

Issue 348: March 9th 2002

A man from Last Chance, Texas, who was diagnosed with a fatal brain tumour decided to finish it quickly by shooting himself in the head. A friend found him lying in a pool of blood and called an ambulance. Not only has he recovered from his injury, but doctors say that he will now lead a normal life, having shot the tumour right out of his brain.

Issue 355: April 27th 2002

An American man has devised a foolproof plan to ensure that his relatives visit his grave after his death. Grover Chestnut, of Montana, has left instructions for an ATM machine to be installed in his headstone. The machine will be programmed to dispense $300 once a week to each of his heirs.

Issue 372: August 24th 2002

Hundreds of people have been injured in an annual stone-throwing festival in central India. About 600 people were hurt, nine of them seriously, during the ancient ritual at the village of Pandhurna in which rival villagers hurl stones at each other across a river. Officials had provided 10,000 rubber balls to minimise injuries, but once they were used up villagers reverted to stones.

Issue 375: Sept 14th 2002

A Romanian who has been run over eight times says he has "had enough". Nicolae Tabacu, 44, has been hit by a train, a bus, a motorcycle and five cars – breaking almost every bone in his body. In his most recent accident, he was run over by a police car, breaking his leg. "Someone up there loves me," said Tabacu. "But I wish the car had hit me harder as I am fed up with hospitals."
Issue 377: Sept 27th 2002

Dutch undertakers in the town of Haarlem have found a way to lighten the mood at funerals – they've hired a clown. Roelof van Wijngaarden says his antics help mourners to let go of their grief. "Imagine following the coffin to the burial place," he said. "It's all very solemn. Then imagine this clown whispering to the children and letting out a fart. The children giggle and then their parents smile – they love it."
Issue 382: Nov 2nd 2002

A Chicago woman has died after being suffocated by her 52F breasts. Angelica Vitadonna, 47, died when she fell out of bed and her mammaries knocked her out. "It was a freak accident," said a policeman. "Her enormous breasts fell down over her face in such a way that she couldn't breathe."
Issue 389: Dec 21st 2002

A chef in a Zurich hotel who lost his finger while operating a meat-slicer submitted a claim to his insurance company. The company was suspicious, and sent an inspector to check the machine. When he turned it on, he too lost his finger. The claim has been approved.
Issue 393: Jan 25th 2003

A Louisiana family visited their bedridden grandmother several times over the course of a month, but failed to notice one crucial factor: she was dead. The family admits they visited Mabel Spurlock, 86, on a regular basis, but didn't noticing anything wrong. Police, who found her decayed remains last week, say she had been dead for at least three weeks.
Issue 395: Feb 8th 2003

A group of Russian train conductors have been hospitalised after repeatedly banging their heads against a train window. To pass the time on a 3,000-mile journey from Novosibirsk to Vladivostok, the conductors staged a contest to find out who had the strongest head. But midway through the journey the crew stopped the train and requested medical help.
Issue 406: April 26th 2003

Two pensioners died after a dancer jumped out of a cake at an old people's home in Perth, Australia. Roger Thornton, 86, and Margaret Flinch, 91, suffered massive heart attacks when Elizabeth 'Boom Boom' Baker burst out of the cake, revealing her "tremendous bust". The cake was meant to be delivered to a stag party being held nearby, but the postman misread the address.
Issue 424: August 30th 2003

A man who woke up from a prostate operation to find his penis had been removed has been awarded undisclosed damages from a hospital in Texas. Hurshell Ralls, 67, sued the surgeons for $3 million.
Issue 425: Sept 6th 2003

A group of interns in a hospital A&E were so flustered when a patient had a heart attack that they borrowed a man's mobile phone and dialled 999. The young doctors were at the end of their first 24-hour shift at the St Paul Hospital in Auckland, New Zealand, when they panicked. "It's not the response we would have wanted," said a hospital spokesman.
Issue 428: Sept 27th 2003

Mourners at an Indian funeral got a nice surprise when the deceased sprang to life just as he was about to be cremated. Mr Velusamy, 80, was awakened by a Hindu ritual in which the corpse is bathed in cold water before being put on the funeral pyre. "It's very cold," he said as he got up from the ground, to the cheers of his family and friends.
Issue 436: Nov 22nd 2003

A 38-year-old Australian dentist blew his nose with such force that he expelled 60% of the frontal lobe of his brain through his sinuses. When paramedics arrived, Marc Tyrier of Brisbane was already dead. "This is definitely one for the books," said the editor of the medical journal Anomalous Deaths.
Issue 457: April 24th 2004

A cemetery in Chile is putting panic buttons in its coffins to stop people being buried alive. Clients at the Camino a Canaan cemetery in Santiago can choose a coffin with a sensor that detects any movement inside. "We want to avoid catalepsy cases, in which a person is paralysed for a few hours and ends up buried as if they were dead," said a spokesman.
Issue 459: May 8th 2004

A Chinese man was hospitalised after using his umbrella as a parachute. The man from Chongqing, western China, jumped from the window of his second floor flat because he thought his microwave was about to explode. He presumed the umbrella would enable him to land safely like Mary Poppins in the Disney film, but was taken to hospital with two broken legs.
Issue 465: June 19th 2004

An attempt to set a new world record for fire-walking has ended in disaster. Of the 341 volunteers who walked across a 12ft pit of hot coals in Dunedin, New Zealand, 28 needed medical attention. The £350 they had raised for the city hospital had to be spent on treating their burns. To top it off, the Guinness Book of Records then informed them that their suffering was all in vain: the fire-walking record is judged on distance, not on numbers taking part.
Issue 469: July 17th 2004

Polish doctors treating a man for headaches were alarmed to find a five-inch knife embedded in his neck. Leonard Woronowicz, 61, had fallen over a stool in his kitchen, knocked himself out, and woken up with a gash in his neck. "I didn't make much of it," he said. "I didn't even guess what had happened the next day, when I couldn't find the kitchen knife". But when he went to hospital a few days later, suffering from recurrent headaches, doctors discovered the missing utensil. It had penetrated his neck without touching any major bones or arteries, and has done no lasting damage.
Issue 502: March 12th 2005

A Russian gun salesman is recovering in hospital after accidentally shooting himself in the head. The deputy manager of the shop in Novosibirsk was joking around with a customer and put a Strazhnik 461 to his head to demonstrate its trigger action. He had forgotten that it was loaded. Luckily, the bullets were made of rubber, and his injuries were not life-threatening.
Issue 503: March 19th 2005

A Romanian doctor is being treated for shock after being punched by a corpse. Bogdan Georgescu, 16, had been taken to the morgue after he collapsed and showed no signs of life. But the doctor saw him stir and came over to investigate. "I saw a dead woman on either side of me, and a man coming towards me in a white coat," the teenager later apologised. "I just panicked." The doctor has been given time off to recover from his ordeal.
Issue 513: May 28th 2005

Two Romanian pensioners were hospitalised after coming to blows over the remote control. Victor Gavrilas, 73, needed an operation after Gheorghe Botezatu, 85, broke his nose during a fight in the TV room of their retirement home. "They've always been one against the other," says Dr Lidia Mihailovii, who runs the home. "Most of the time they quarrel about the TV. This time they hit each other with their walking sticks." Mr Botezatu, who has previously been caught smuggling in alcohol and trying to have sex with the female residents, has been warned he will be expelled if there is any more trouble.
Issue 522: July 30th 2005

A British man who dozed off by a rock pool while on holiday in Fiji awoke to find a barnacle clamped to his manhood. He rushed straight to the nearest hospital, where an attractive female nurse tried to prise the shell off. But as his admiration for the nurse started to show, the shell tightened its grip. A male nurse had to be summoned to take over. The holidaymaker claimed £50 from his insurance company to compensate for his distress.
Issue 532: Oct 8th 2005

A traffic warden in Maroondah, Australia, issued a ticket to an illegally parked car without noticing that the driver was slumped over the steering wheel – dead. The town mayor, Paul Denham, apologised to the family of the deceased 71-year-old man, and explained that the warden had approached the car from the passenger side. "He did not notice anything unusual regarding the vehicle, and is extremely distressed to have learned of the situation."
Issue 536: Nov 5th 2005

A Dutch entrepreneur is offering a new extreme sport – "fun burials". For 75 Euros an hour, Eddy Daams will bury you in a coffin five feet underground, with a 3.5 tonne concrete block on top. Each coffin is equipped with an oxygen supply, a panic button and a webcam to allow friends to watch. Mr Daams, who runs the project from his garden in Eexterveen, says: "It is very safe, nothing can go wrong."
Issue 546: Jan 21st 2006

A circus dwarf came to an unfortunate end after being swallowed by a hippopotamus in a freak accident in Thailand. The dwarf, known as Od, bounced sideways from a trampoline and was swallowed by a yawning hippo waiting to appear in the next act. More than 1,000 spectators continued to applaud before realising there had been a tragic mistake.
Issue 550: Feb 18th 2006

THE YOUNG TONY BLAIR

The Corridors of Power

American men with famous wives have started a club called The Dennis Thatcher Society. Their motto is "Yes dear!" and they meet for dinner once a year.
Issue 21: Oct 21st 1995

Carlos Menem, President of Argentina, has sent French president Jacques Chirac a present of two horses trained to dance the tango.
Issue 40: March 2nd 1996

John Weintraub's obsession with collecting plastic figurines of US presidents – included as free gifts in packets of Happy Morning Muesli – has landed him in jail. After two years he had the whole set except for Thomas Jefferson. "I'd bought hundreds of damn packets but he was never in them." Mr Weintraub was so desperate that he broke into a cereal factory and opened every Happy Morning box he could find. He was spotted by a guard, arrested and jailed. "It's OK though," he said, "because at my first prison breakfast out popped a Jefferson."
Issue 143: March 7th 1998

A Republican candidate for the House of Representatives who wrote and appeared in a soft-porn film says it shows that he is "a communicator". The film features naked women lathering themselves with motor oil. "It's as tasteful as it can get with naked women in it," said the candidate, Harold Gunn.
Issue 247: March 18th 2000

The Queen is taking 20 tons of luggage with her on her two-week tour of Australia, according to The Sun, including her own luxury lavatory seat and paper.
Issue 247: March 18th 2000

Bill Clinton has developed a hopeless crush on Wonder Woman, says the National Enquirer. Lynda Carter, star of the Seventies TV hit, has become a regular visitor to the White House, and the president is said to be so smitten by her "entrancing blue eyes" that he is "afraid to be alone with her". At a recent dinner, he called her "Wonder Woman" all night, and they spent ages "talking quietly" together. "He really is trying to be careful these day," said a source, "but he just can't help himself."
Issue 272: Sept 9th 2000

George W. Bush had better watch out, says The Fortean Times. The US president, elected last year, may face the curse of the "0". Since 1840, every president elected in a year ending in a zero has either died, or been shot, while in office. William Henry Harrison, Abraham Lincoln, James Garfield, William McKinley, Warren G. Harding, Franklin D. Roosevelt, John F. Kennedy and Ronald Reagan all won elections in "0" years. Of these, only Reagan, who was shot in 1981, survived the curse.
Issue 301: April 7th 2001

Steve Bracks, premier of the Australian state of Victoria, paid consultants £10,500 for advice on how to make his office more efficient. They told him to keep a pad on his desk for jotting down telephone messages.
Issue 304: April 28th 2001

The Chinese have found a new way to ridicule George W. Bush. The latest craze sweeping the nation is the Porta-Bush – a toy similar to a Tamagotchi. Players get to feed, clothe and discipline the president, as well as helping him make vital decisions such as whether to bomb Britney Spears.
Issue 304: April 28th 2001

Californian Cable TV presenter Emily Hofsetter was so appalled by George W. Bush's election victory that she shaved off her pubic hair and posted it to the new President. "We need direct action," she told viewers, "so I'm urging all those who believe in democracy to join my 'I'd Rather Go Bare Than Have a Bush' campaign."
Issue 306: May 12th 2001

On his second day with the company, an employee of the Automobile Association decided to snoop into some celebrity files. When he discovered Tony Blair's details, he altered his name to "Mr Saddam Hussein – aka Twatface", only to discover he couldn't change it back again. After "a huge probe" to track the guilty party, the company has now fired him.
Issue 326: Sept 29th 2001

A Croatian parliamentary session was halted after an MP told a female colleague: "God created you as mattresses and not as wise men."
Issue 329: Oct 20th 2001

A local councillor who agreed to strip for charity at the Royal British Legion Club in Ebbw Vale, south Wales, only got as far as removing his shirt and tie before the audience asked him to stop.
Issue 336: Dec 8th 2001

The Queen missed a royal fly-past in her honour when she got stuck behind a learner driver. HRH was on her way from Sandringham to RAF Marham when she got held up by student Sarah Proctor, driving a Vauxhall Corsa at a snail's pace. "We noticed the Queen was behind us," said instructor Martin Underwood, "but we were observing the correct speed and there was no place to pass."
Issue 356: May 4th 2002

A French councillor stands accused of misappropriating public funds after paying himself £50,000 to write a report on mosquitoes. The report contained such scientific insights as "mosquitoes can be aggressive" and "they have the ability to suck and sting".
Issue 368: July 27th 2002

La Cicciolina, the Italian porn star turned politician, is prepared to make the ultimate sacrifice for world peace, says the Daily Star: she'll have sex with Saddam Hussein. The blonde provocateur has reiterated the offer she first made during the Gulf War, promising to bed the Iraqi dictator if he'll co-operate with the West. "I would do it holding my nose and closing my eyes," she says. "I would do it for peace."
Issue 379: Oct 12th 2002

An Indonesian businessman who spent two years bribing local councillors is demanding his money back after they failed to elect him governor of Jakarta. Mahfudz Djaelani says he spent 200 million rupiah (£14,000) bribing 40 city councillors, and billions entertaining them, yet only received three votes. "I want the money back or I will reveal their names," says Djaelani. "The winner must have given more money than I did."
Issue 380: Oct 19th 2002

A Belgian mayor has set up a Department of Tenderness to encourage people to be nicer to each other. Antoine Denert, mayor of Kruibeke, said he hoped international organisations would follow his example. "People don't cuddle any more and that's why there are so many conflicts," he said. "I will set an example and start in my own village by caressing, cuddling and kissing as many people as possible."
Issue 403: April 5th 2003

US soldiers claim to have found remnants of Saddam Hussein's moustache in the rubble of a Baghdad restaurant. The "scorched whiskers" were uncovered in the ruins of the al-Sa'ah restaurant, which was destroyed in an air strike on 7 April after US intelligence claimed the dictator was dining there. A military source has revealed that the facial hair contains traces of hummus and hot peppers – Saddam's favourite dish, which he always had specially prepared for him. The moustache is currently undergoing DNA testing.
Issue 413: June 14th 2003

Russian popsters Tatu have big ambitions. The lesbian duo have announced their intention of running against Vladimir Putin in the March presidential election. Although candidates have to be over 35, Yulia Volkova, 18 and Lena Katina, 19, will run as joint candidates with a combined age of 37.
Issue 442: Jan 10th 2004

An Italian mayor is offering to pay for councillors to have plastic surgery, to improve the image of the town. Sandro Donati, mayor of Mulazzo, Tuscany, has put aside more than £2,000 to cover emergency "beauty treatment" for politicians. He came up with the idea after one councillor asked for a contribution towards her blue contact lenses. "Another asked for money to pay for a tanning session," says Donati, "and others are filing requests for surgery to make them look more charming."
Issue 447: Feb 14th 2004

An Indian man is hoping to break records at this year's parliamentary election – by becoming the world's least successful electoral candidate. Ajit Kumar Jain, of Madhya Pradesh, has stood as an independent in seven national, nine state and seven civic elections. He has spent £3.84 on this campaign, which he runs from a handcart with the slogan: "Ensure my defeat with the minimum number of votes."
Issue 459: May 8th 2004

A Dutch MP is calling for unsolicited toe-licking to be made a criminal offence. The move follows the release of a man who was arrested for licking women's toes while they were sunbathing in a Rotterdam park. Police had to release the man without charge because toe-licking isn't a crime in Holland. Peter van Heemst, an MP for the PVDA party, says: "It's an insult to privacy and integrity when someone licks another person's toes when he is not asked to."
Issue 473: August 14th 2004

Viktor Yanukovich, the Ukrainian prime minister, is resorting to desperate measures to win this month's general election: voters in the city of Donetsk are being offered free stripteases. One of Yanukovich's campaign team, who helped organise the free strip nights at the Santa Fe bar, explained: "We hope the voters will remember who gave them this show when they go to the ballot box.'
Issue 483: Oct 23rd 2004

Cherie Blair has lost none of her faith in alternative therapies, reports the Daily Mail. Mrs Blair, 50, has reportedly been making regular visits to a former estate agent, Lilias Curtin, who practices "thought field therapy" in Fulham, west London. Mrs Curtin attended London's College of Psychic Studies in the Nineties, before setting up her business, Full of Energy Ltd. She claims to be able to cure grief, insomnia, panic attacks and even jealousy – sometimes in minutes – by tapping certain points on the body in a special sequence.
Issue 492: Dec 24th 2004

There are more than 20 independent "nations" within Australia, founded by eccentrics wanting to break away from the government. They include the Hutt River Province in Western Australia, ruled by Prince Leonard and Princess Shirley; the Empire of Atlantium, located in the one-bedroom Sydney apartment of George Cruickshank; and the Gay and Lesbian Kingdom of the Coral Sea – an archipelago of tiny, uninhabited coral islands ruled over by His Majesty Emperor Dale.
Issue 501: March 5th

A German Prince has taken out a lonely hearts ad to find a princess willing to become his bride. Prince Ruediger of Saxony, the great-grandson of the last King of Saxony, has a 30-bedroom stately home and his own forest in Mortizburg. His newspaper ad reads: "Genuine Prince, sweet-natured and industrious, is seeking after much disappointment a decent woman aged between 25 and 50 for marriage. Pocket money of 2,500 euros a month." Although the ideal candidate would be from Saxony, Prince Ruediger, 51, says he is prepared to consider members of the British royal family.
Issue 514: June 4th 2005

A bar of soap made from the Italian prime minister's fat has gone on display at an art gallery in Basle, Switzerland. The artist, Gianni Motti, 47, claims to have bought the fat from an employee at the Swiss clinic where Berlusconi reportedly had liposuction. "It was jelly-like and stank, like butter gone off or old chip pan oil," says Motti. He hopes to sell the work, entitled Clean Hands, for £10,000.
Issue 516: June 18th 2005

Bill Clinton's official visit to Kenya, which began last week, is particularly exciting for local councillor Godwin Kipkemoi Chepkurgor, who has business to discuss with the former president. In 2000, Chepkurgor wrote to Clinton, offering him 20 cattle and 40 goats in return for his daughter Chelsea's hand in marriage. While patiently waiting for a reply, Chepkurgor has been following Chelsea's progress through the media. "The last I heard of her was that she had graduated from the prestigious Oxford University and she was going on holiday," he says.
Issue 523: August 6th 2005

A man tried to enrol in a school in Minnesota by posing as a teenage member of the British royal family. Caspian Crichton-Stuart IV, Duke of Cleveland and Earl of Scooby, said he was 27th in line to the throne and friends with Prince Harry. But students discovered he was in fact a 22-year-old sex offender called Joshua Gardner. "Why would a member of the royal family come to Minnesota to go to school?" said Matt Murphy, editor of the school paper.
Issue 547: Jan 28th 2006

Destiny Calling

Police were forced to rescue three fortune-tellers from an angry mob in Bulgaria after they predicted that flying saucers would land, bringing with them £8billion. The saucers failed to show up.
Issue 18: Sept 23rd 1995

An Australian insurance worker with psychic powers is suing her boss for £20,000 because, she claims, he is going to sexually harass her in the future.
Issue 35: Jan 27th 1996

Two groups of clairvoyants arranged rival psychic fairs on the same day, a few miles apart at Cliftonville and Ramsgate in Kent. "It was due to unforeseen circumstances," said an organiser.
Issue 46: April 13th 1996

Mystic Arnold Kosner is making a fortune by reading women's bottoms. For £50, Kosner, of Tilburg, Holland, smears their buttocks with paint, gets them to sit on a piece of paper, studies the imprint and then tells them their future.
Issue 153: May 16th 1998

Fortune teller Maria Scivolone of Verona, Italy, is being sued after failing to predict that her crystal ball would fall off her balcony on to a passer-by's head.
Issue 157: June 13th 1998

Mystic Nayir Bagnar, 63, of Poona, India, atoned for sins in a past life by pushing a radish 209 miles with his nose.
Issue 171: Sept 19th 1998

Michael Burns, 84, has returned home to New Zealand after spending over 60 years in the foothills of Mount Everest waiting for the world to end. Burns made the headlines in 1938 when he predicted the world's imminent oblivion by flood and fled to the hills of Nepal believing only those on the highest mountains would survive. The hermit, who is now living with his niece, said: "I've completely wasted my life."
Issue 213: July 17th 1999

Dr Anna Furundzija, an expert in telekinesis, says she has lost her three-year-old daughter, Charity, after trying to teleport her from Manhattan to her father's apartment in Tokyo. "Charity could be stranded on any spot on the globe – or light years away on the Dog Star Sirius," she wept. Dr Elizero Murhof of Sweden's International Parapsychological Institute has assembled the world's top psychics, clairvoyants and astral travellers in a bid to find the young girl.
Issue 286: Dec 16th 2000

Brittney Pringle, a nine-month-old baby from Perth, Australia, made her parents rich the moment she spoke her first words. "Brittney gave us a couple of goo-goos and ga-gas and then blurted out the numbers 9, 12, 14, 22, 31 and 39," says proud mum Dorcas Pringle. "We ran out and bought a lottery ticket – and now our Brittney's going to grow up as the world's youngest self-made millionaire. I can't explain how she did what she did, but we are determined she's going to lead a normal life."
Issue 290: Jan 20th 2001

An American housewife is offering psychic consultations to troubled pets. Carol Schultz, who claims she can speak the language of animals, charges $50 a session to counsel cats, dogs and horses. Satisfied clients include a dog which was Hitler in a past life and slept all the time to escape depression, and a dog which was trapped in a cat's body.
Issue 341: Jan 19th 2002

The Center For UFO Studies has compiled a list of 13,528 American women who believe that they have been abducted by aliens. Of these, 1,501 report that their underwear has been kept by the aliens.
Issue 369: August 3rd 2002

The Chinese are planning a national jump to stop a giant asteroid colliding with earth. Scientists tracking the asteroid say it could hit the globe on Friday 21 March, 2014, causing a return to the Ice Age. But the Chinese hope that if all 1.5 billion of them join in "the Great Leap of Loving Mankind and Saving the Earth Initiative" they could nudge the Earth out of harm's way.
Issue 430: Oct 11th 2003

A Russian teenager who claims to have X-ray vision has developed a huge following of "patients". Doctors are at a loss to explain how 16-year-old Natalia Demkina can diagnose illnesses in the human body with her naked eye. Natalia, who comes from Saransk, 400 miles east of Moscow, first demonstrated this talent aged ten. "I told my mum I could see what her inner organs looked like," she recalls. Her mother took her to a psychiatrist, but she drew a picture of his stomach which revealed a previously undiagnosed ulcer. Since then, she has correctly diagnosed dozens of cases. "I am a traditional doctor and did not believe her claims," says senior consultant Irina Kachan. "But I must admit the girl has an outstanding talent."
Issue 444: Jan 24th 2004

Officials in Norway have agreed not to demolish a dilapidated old barn, for fear of disturbing its spectral occupants. "There are under-world creatures living in that barn," said its owner. "Many years ago, I removed its roof. I had several encounters with the under-world and fell gravely ill." The local council has heeded his warning, and decided the barn should stay.
Issue 487: Nov 20th 2004

A Russian astrologer is suing Nasa for disrupting her horoscope readings. Nasa scientists were delighted this week when they successfully crashed their Deep Impact probe into a comet known as Tempel 1. But astrologer Marina Bai says she will have to rewrite all her horoscopes to take into account the altered orbit of the comet, and is demanding $300m in damages. "It is obvious that elements of the comet's orbit, and correspondingly the ephemeris, will change after the explosion," Ms Bai explained.
Issue 519: July 9th 2005

My name is actually **Stan** — The Bible had already gone to press before we noticed the misprint...

Pemsau

Oooops

A Paris chef fed up with an awkward customer served him a beer mat, marinated in wine and fried in batter, as a veal escalope. The diner, according to the Daily Star, enjoyed the veal but complained about the vegetables.
Issue 11: August 5th 1995

An American pilot had to make a grovelling apology after landing 200 miles off-course. "Gee! Sorry, wrong country," he told the 241 passengers after landing in Belgium instead of Germany. The cabin crew on the Northwest Airlines flight from Detroit knew they were off course but did nothing because they assumed they were being hi-jacked.
Issue 20: Oct 7th 1995

When Bradley Plumster of Vermont decided to spend a week living as a prehistoric man in local woods, hunstmen mistook him for a giant beaver and began shooting, despite his cries of: "No, no ! I'm a man!" After pursuing him the finally shot him in the leg. "He was lucky," said a hunter. "We only let him live because talking beavers are so rare."
Issue 95: March 29th 1997

A busload of Zimbabwean psychiatric patients on their way to hospital escaped when their driver stopped for a drink. Returning to an empty bus, he panicked, picked up passengers from an ordinary bus stop and drove them to hospital, telling staff they were "excitable and prone to inventing stories". It was three days before the commuters were released.
Issue 107 June 21st 1997

Spanish "business motivation" lecturer Manuel Torres is being sued for £2 million after giving firm handshake lessons in Madrid during which he broke 32 people's fingers.
Issue 125: Oct 25th 1997

Susan Beal of Bexleyheath, Kent, was stunned when she received a letter from Dixons addressed to Mrs U.G.L. Fat Cow. The letter, which began "Dear Mrs Fat Cow", was signed by the Quality Standards Director. When Mrs Beal complained an assistant told her: "Plenty of customers answer to the name Fat Cow." A spokesman for the electrical store said the letter, inviting Mrs Beal to take out an extended warranty on a TV, was an internal joke and shouldn't have been sent.
Issue 138: Jan 31st 1998

Wendall Egthrob almost died after getting trapped inside his thief-resistant greenhouse. Mr Egthrob, 56, of Perth, Australia, was tending his tomatoes when the "heavy-duty door" slammed shut. No one heard his screams through the bullet-proof glass. Trapped for two days, he sweated off almost 20lb in weight. "I'm not only thinner, but two inches taller," he said. "These greenhouses really make you sprout."
Issue 138: Jan 31st 1998

Kasuo Hekaharo's blow-up underpants caused havoc on a rush-hour tube in Japan. Hekaharo, 43, designed the rubber pants to inflate to 30 times their normal size in the event of a tidal wave. "I've always been scared of drowning, and I wear them 24 hours a day," he explained. Alas, they accidentally inflated on a packed train, squashing all around him before someone punctured the pants with a pen.
Issue 142: Feb 28th 1998

A chef deep-fried a customer's mobile phone after another diner complained about its incessant ringing. Lawrence Clifford, a chef at The Gallery restaurant in Ipswich, took the £250 phone when the businessman went to the lavatory. He then dipped it in batter, cooked it in boiling oil and served it to the owner with chips and salad.
Issue 155: May 30th 1998

French burglar Joseph N'dai was arrested after being flattened by a giant ear. N'dai was robbing an ear specialist when he was discovered by the resident doctor. In a bid to block his getaway, the doctor flung a plaster-of-paris demonstration ear from the window, scoring a direct hit. "I shall be suing," fumed the thief. "That ear has seriously affected my hearing."
Issue 159: June 27th

A teddy bears' tea party for 200 children in Australia ended in chaos after an inebriated teddy bear flew his microlight aircraft into a tree. Alan Woom, 41, of Adelaide, was to have been the highlight of the party as he performed his flyover, dressed as Winnie the Pooh and waving at the children below. Unfortunately, the drunken pilot chose to dive-bomb the children instead, screaming "Winnie's going to get ya!" at the top of his voice. Minutes later, he crashed into a tree, breaking both his legs. "Pooh Bear used to be my son's hero," said one angry mother, "but now whenever he's mentioned he wets his bed."

Issue 170: Sept 12th 1998

Giuseppe Plantini of Bologna failed his driving test because of his superstitious mother. When Magdalena Plantini realised she hadn't wished him luck, she went charging off to the test centre. Her son had already left but she caught up with him with his car on a dual carriageway, where she pulled alongside him and screamed: "Good luck, my Giuseppe". Distracted, he lost control of the wheel, slammed into a wall and broke the examiner's legs.

Issue 174: Oct 10th 1998

Pensioner Alf France got a shock when he went to post a letter in Wrexham, North Wales and a hand came out to take it. A voice then cried: "Help! Get me out of here!" The local mailman had been trapped inside for 25 minutes after a gust of wind shut the door of the king-sized box.

Issue 178: Nov 7th 1998

Two drivers in Germany, peering from their side windows in fog, fractured their skulls when their heads clashed together.

Issue 183: Dec 12th 1998

Anton Stoikich, 38, of Sofia, Bulgaria, went into hospital to have a bunion removed and came out with 34DD silicone breasts after his trolley got mixed up with that of a man having a sex change. "The doctors were very insensitive," he complained. "They just said: 'We've made a bit of a boob.'"

Issue 185: Jan 2nd 1999

Twins Luke and John Ladell, 17, passed their driving tests on the same day in Cumbria, then crashed into each other on their way home from the test centre.

Issue 200: April 17th 1999

Members of an all-girl biker gang are suing a tattoo artist for writing the wrong message on their breasts, says The Star. Dennis LaRoux was asked to write Satan's Slaves on the three girls' bosoms but misheard and wrote Stan's Slaves instead. "Mad Shirl" Haddon is demanding $250,000 in compensation. "It's totally humiliating," she said. "It looks as if the three of us are seeing a man called Stan."
Issue 210: June 26th 1999

Actors in Virginia who were enacting the history of slavery for tourists had to abandon their play after repeated attacks. White actors, playing slave traders, kept being punched by enraged onlookers. One tourist even tried to drum up a revolt, yelling, "There are only three of them and a hundred of us!" before disarming a slave trader of his musket. The performance was abandoned when a group of children formed a human chain around a slave, following him on his lunch break and to the lavatory.
Issue 214: July 24th 1999

Maria Nascimento, a mother-of-seven, burned her £50,000 winning lottery ticket after a church minister in Brazil said she would go to hell if she took the "devil's money". Meanwhile, her compatriot Gloria Mendes literally died of excitement after her husband slipped her a bogus lottery ticket for $45 million. "I'll never forgive myself – never," said Enrique Mendes, 55. "Gloria was a lottery fanatic... and I couldn't resist playing a little prank. My only consolation is knowing she died happy."
Issue 218: August 21st 1999

An American guest who was booked into a London hotel sent a fax querying the WC1 postcode: "Does it mean you only have one toilet?"
Issue 218: August 21st 1999

A motorist wrecked his car after a sneeze sent his false teeth smashing through the windscreen. Hans Auflann, 78, sneezed while driving past a rape field near Seigen, Germany. "My false teeth came flying out and smashed the windshield," said Hans, "I couldn't see a thing and drove into a lamppost. The car is a write-off."
Issue 220: Sept 4th 1999

Artist Jordan McKenzie, who showed students a film of himself cavorting naked with a broom handle up his bottom, has agreed to leave his job as a lecturer at the Cheltenham and Gloucester College of Higher Education.
Issue 230: Nov 13th 1999

Syd Johnson, a DIY fanatic from Ipswich, Suffolk, has vowed to continue using his treasured power saws even though he keeps chopping off bits of himself. The accident-prone carpenter has already sliced through a leg, chopped off two fingers and a thumb and sawed through his left arm. Syd, 68, said: "The doctors have suggested I give up DIY. But no way."
Issue 233: Dec 4th 1999

The land-locked country Swaziland has lost its entire merchant navy. The fleet, which consists of just one ship, has completely disappeared. But Transport Minister Ephraem Magagula is not worried: "The situation is absolutely under control. We believe it is in the sea somewhere," he told the Johannesburg Star. "At one time we sent a team of men to look for it but there was a problem with drink and they failed to find it. But I categorically reject all suggestions of incompetence on the part of this government. The Swazimar is a big ship painted in the sort of nice bright colours you can see at night. Mark my words, it will turn up."
Issue 237: Jan 8th 2000

Opera-lover Fred Harrop was surprised when friends sent him a book of pornographic photographs for his 80th birthday. The internet book service Amazon.com had mistakenly sent him Literate Smut instead of Backstage at the Opera with Cecilia Bartoli. Amazon has apologised for the error, and also for a remark by a company spokesman who told Harrop's friends: "If you think Mr Harrop was disappointed, imagine how the guy who got the opera book feels."
Issue 240: Jan 29th 2000

A woman who phoned the Brighton police to say she had found a hole in the road was put through to the lost property department.
Issue 241: Feb 5th 2000

A BBC producer was run over by an 85-year-old woman while filming a Panorama report about the dangers posed to pedestrians by reckless motorists. Rachel Morgan was conducting an interview with a local at Britain's worst accident blackspot, in Yeovil, Somerset, when a Nissan hatchback drove round the corner and struck her down. But the incident will not be used in the programme, which concerns accidents caused by speeding. The granny was driving at a sedate 15mph.
Issue 242: Feb 12th 2000

Frenchman Robert Alois made £125,000 at the roulette table in Monte Carlo. But this had nothing to do with his gambling skills. He was awarded the money in compensation after a steel ball flew off the wheel and hit him in the eye.
Issue 244: Feb 26th 2000

An Anglesey vet was struck off after farmers complained that he was too drunk to treat their livestock. Meredydd Jones diagnosed sunstroke for a cow suffering from food poisoning, and confirmed that a horse had been killed by lightning without even leaving his car to take a look. Jones denied he was drunk, claiming the smell of booze was the spirit he used to wash his hands after he'd castrated a pair of bulls.
Issue 246: March 11th 2000

Fritz Gruber, 33, was cleaning a rifle in his flat in Ulm, Germany, when it went off, blowing a hole in the ceiling and wounding a burglar in the apartment upstairs.
Issue 250: April 8th 2000

Detroit airport was put on red-alert when a man boarding a plane greeted the pilot – whom he knew – with the words "Hi Jack". Air-traffic controllers listening in the airport tower ordered armed Swat teams to board the plane, before realising their mistake. "Now they'll probably pass a rule that no-one named Jack can ever be hired in aviation again," said police captain Chuck Jehle.
Issue 260: June 17th 2000

Police arrested nine men for fighting after a bikini-clad woman walked into a bar in Turin and promised to make love to the strongest.
Issue 263: July 8th 2000

When an unnamed woman in Durrington, West Sussex, heard strange drilling sounds outside her house, she dialled 999, fearing burglars were raiding a local building site. The police rushed round but found nothing suspicious. The noise was eventually traced to the caller's bedside cabinet where her vibrator had gone off.
Issue 273: Sept 16th 2000

A deaf and dumb man at a hostel in Blackburn was arrested after a member of staff translated the torrent of abuse he was giving in sign language to police officers.
Issue 276: Oct 7th 2000

Four British schoolboys have been cleared of terrorism. The boys, aged ten and 11, from Thorpe House School in Buckinghamshire, had sent a Christmas message to the Clintons reading: "Send me a million dollars or I will blow up the White House", followed by another, half an hour later, reading: "I still have not received my million dollars. It is now $2 million or I will blow up Texas." An FBI agent promptly appeared at their school to interview the headmaster, but not before the boys had received an automated reply from the White House thanking them for contacting the president.
Issue 293: Feb 10th 2001

An undercover reporter for the News of the World got a job as a porter to investigate conditions at a north London hospital. On his first day, he was introduced to a fellow worker, also recently appointed, who would show him what to do. The reporter immediately recognised his new colleague – an undercover reporter from the Sunday Mirror.
Issue 298: March 17th 2001

It isn't easy running a British tourism company. The annual report of the Holiday Cottage Company describes a litany of troublesome tourists, including a woman who complained that people kept staring at her when she stood naked in the garden, and a Chinese family that insisted on having a pond with ducks. They then shot and ate the unlucky birds.
Issue 304: April 28th 2001

At the age of 82, Shulamit Dezhin from Asdad, Israel, has at last passed her driving test after failing 35 times. She needed a licence in order to visit her parents in Israel, but she has taken so long to get it that they are now both dead.
Issue 309: June 2nd 2001

Ethiopian Gazehegn Debebe, who complained of stomach-ache, is feeling better after doctors removed 222 rusty nails from his stomach. Debebe had swallowed the nails along with a collection of keys and coins. "He's never been fussy about food," said his mother, "but we had no idea he was eating metal."
Issue 313: June 30th 2001

A hospital visitor who asked doctors whether she could smoke on the ward was told it was bad for her health. So she leant out of the window for a crafty puff – and fell 60ft into a tree. Inge Brunner, 25, who was visiting a friend at Tübingen hospital, Germany, escaped serious injury. "I'm going to give up smoking straight away," she said.
Issue 319: August 11th 2001

Firemen in Brazil accidentally torched 7,500 acres of land while trying to teach farmers how to control agricultural burning.
Issue 321: August 25th 2001

The Democratic Republic of the Congo has discovered that 21,652 civil servants on its payroll do not exist.
Issue 326: Sept 29th 2001

Southend-on-Sea is having second thoughts about its new traffic warden uniforms. It has received several complaints about wardens strutting the streets with the initials SS emblazoned on their shoulders.
Issue 327: Oct 6th 2001

New Zealand's Green Party recently agreed to support a ban on dihydrogen monoxide, after concerned citizen Phil Gully informed them that it was a chemical "used in nuclear power stations, commonly found in pre-cancerous cells and present in acid rain". Its more common name is water.
Issue 331: Nov 3rd 2001

A statue kept in the basement of a Southampton museum has been identified as a priceless 2,700-year-old Egyptian mummy. Staff had been using it as a cycle rack.
Issue 331: Nov 3rd 2001

In an attempt to seem Westernised, a department store in Japan mounted an extravagant Christmas display, featuring a life-sized Santa Claus – crucified on a cross.
Issue 339: Jan 5th 2002

A woman got stuck to an aeroplane lavatory seat when she pressed the high-pressure vacuum flush while still seated. She was only freed when the Scandinavian Airlines flight landed in the US.
Issue 342: Jan 26th 2002

A weighing machine has been removed from a shopping centre after telling a woman to "get off, fat pig". It was one of many similar comments printed out by the scales in Greensborough Plaza, Melbourne, Australia. The supplier believes someone tampered with the machine after gaining access to a hidden keypad.
Issue 342: Jan 26th 2002

A tram was derailed in Manchester after running over a bundle of newspapers bearing the headline: 'Rail misery is getting worse.'
Issue 343: Feb 2nd 2002

A British-born chemist who felt that his life lacked excitement broke into an elderly colleague's house to steal her underwear, a court in Brisbane, Australia, heard last week. Dr Ronald Mellow, 53, filled a pillowcase with stockings, bras, knickers, nightwear and shoes stolen from the 64-year-old woman whose keys he'd had copied. The former government scientist was foiled by a neighbour, who pushed Mellow's head through a cupboard door and sat on him until police arrived. "He is acutely embarrassed," said Mellow's lawyer in his defence, "and he has already suffered some punishment by having his head pushed through a door."
Issue 345: Feb 16th 2002

A Jerusalem woman tried to kill a cockroach by flushing it down the loo and emptying a can of powerful insecticide into the bowl. Her husband threw a cigarette into the loo and it exploded, scorching his nether regions. On hearing how he sustained his injuries, the two stretcher-bearers laughed so much they dropped him down the stairs, breaking his arm.
Issue 348: March 9th 2002

When a trawler sank near Japan recently, the crew claimed it had been damaged by a cow which had fallen out of the sky. No one believed them – except the Russian military. That day, the pilots of a Russian military cargo jet had found a cow wandering on a Siberian airfield and loaded it on board. While cruising at 30,000 feet, the terrified creature ran amok and was expelled from the plane.
Issue 349: March 16th 2002

Turkish Mehmet Esirgen has been shot in the leg by his exasperated son after attempting for a third time to transplant a donkey's penis on to his own.
Issue 353: April 13th 2002

A group of tourists visiting the Chinese imperial city of Xian was beaten up by tour guides dressed as ancient warriors. The tour guides, who were pretending to be warriors from the third Century Qin dynasty, used sticks and clubs to drive off two tourists who were sitting on a bench that was off-limits. When other visitors came to their rescue, a full-scale brawl ensued.
Issue 358: May 18th 2002

An overweight Romanian policeman has resigned in embarrassment after falling into a lavatory. The 18-stone constable fell into a loo at his local pub in the town of Dorohoi when the seat broke under his weight. Cornel Agheorghitoaie, 27, had been on a date with his fiancée when the accident happened. "This is a really small town and everyone was laughing. I had to go," he said.
Issue 361: June 8th 2002

An Argentinian housewife has been arrested for holding a washing machine repairman hostage. Terra Populares, 44, was so enraged by her faulty appliance that she held a gun to the repairman's head and forced him to sign a statement swearing that the machine would never break again.
Issue 372: August 24th 2002

A New Zealand official has been charged with altering a woman's name to Fat Ass on an electoral roll. The victim, Kylene Soar, who is sensitive about her weight, said she was mortified when she opened a letter from the Electoral Enrolment Centre to see that her name had been registered as Kylene Fat Ass. A 23-year-old woman is being prosecuted under the 1993 Electoral Act.
Issue 373: August 31st 2002

A woman who boarded a bus in Darwin, Australia, got the surprise of her life when she took a seat and discovered a crocodile sitting next to her. "I've got no idea where he came from," said bus driver Baz Young. "It's just one of those things that happens in the Northern Territories."
Issue 381: Oct 26th 2002

A Georgian stowaway had a disappointing end to his voyage. Determined to start a new life, Kheshein Zenbadi hid on a ship that was sailing from the former Soviet republic of Georgia to the US. When he thought the ship had docked in America, Zenbadi threw himself into the water, shouting "I'm free". But Zenbadi had actually thrown himself into the Suez Canal, where the ship had stopped to refuel. He is now in the custody of Egyptian naval authorities.
Issue 381: Oct 26th 2002

A doctor treating a ten-year-old American boy discovered a frog in his throat – literally. The boy, who had been camping beside a Louisiana swamp, cut short his holiday after he experienced difficulty swallowing. "It must have hopped into his mouth while he was sleeping," said the doctor.
Issue 384: Nov 16th 2002

A British holidaymaker suffered a blow to his masculine pride when he popped into an Australian pub. The man, who was driving, ordered a low-alcohol beer at the Royal Mail Hotel in the outback. When the bill arrived, it listed "one poofter drink".
Issue 385: Nov 23rd 2002

A Santa Claus has been arrested for dealing drugs in a Florida shopping mall. Don Henkerson, 45, was detained after police found 85 crack rocks in his Santa suit. They became suspicious when an undercover cop overheard teenagers telling Santa they wanted "rocks" and "some of that good shit" for Christmas.
Issue 388: Dec 14th 2002

A Taiwanese woman who was blind for 43 years had her sight miraculously restored when she bumped into a tractor. Miyagu Taitung, 53, says she was stunned when she looked in a mirror and saw how attractive she was. Now she wants a boyfriend: "All my life I assumed I was ugly, but now that I know how beautiful I am, I don't think I'll have too much trouble."
Issue 393: Jan 25th 2003

A circus knife-thrower with a wobbly aim is is looking for a new assistant. Jayde Hanson, who appears with the Cottle and Austen Electric Circus in Exeter, has impaled two assistants in three years – one of them required stitches and the other was convinced he was trying to kill her. "It wasn't that at all," says Hanson. "I just missed. I never want to hurt the girls but my concentration wavers at times."
Issue 396: Feb 15th 2003

Twenty mental patients who were being transported to a hospital in Zimbabwe escaped when their bus driver stopped off at a bar for a drink. Unable to round up the patients, the driver offered free rides to 20 sane people instead. He drove them to the hospital and passed them off as the original patients. When the passengers protested, he told hospital officials they were "excitable" and prone to bizarre fantasies. They finally convinced doctors they were telling the truth three days later.
Issue 400: March 15th 2003

An Exeter man became so fed up with his neighbour's rubbish-strewn garden he decided to report him to his local environmental health officer – only to discover that they were one and the same person. David Chambers' garden contains two rusting cars, a derelict transit van, an abandoned milk float and a bed, but he insists that "it is not a tip".
Issue 401: March 22nd 2003

A reporter who claimed to be filing live radio reports from Baghdad was actually broadcasting from a broom cupboard in Swaziland. Phesheay Dube, who worked for the state radio station, was spotted by MPs sneaking out of a cupboard in the parliamentary building.
Issue 404: April 12th 2003

A Croatian man who escaped seven major disasters has been dubbed the luckiest man alive, after winning the jackpot with his first lottery ticket in 40 years. Frane Selak has survived a train crash, a coach crash and being hit by a bus. He was thrown from a plane, but landed unhurt in a haystack. He escaped from two of his cars before they exploded, and jumped out of another one just before it went over a cliff. Now the 74-year-old has pocketed £600,000 in the state lottery. "I am either the world's unluckiest man," he says, "or the luckiest."
Issue 415: June 28th 2003

An Austrian man who got high on butane gas became so hungry that he ate his toes. The 35-year-old became ravenous after inhaling the gas. Finding nothing to eat in the fridge, he cut off his toes and fried them. When the paramedics arrived, he offered them a toe, saying, "It tastes like chicken."
Issue 415: June 28th 2003

A disgruntled bank customer in Hong Kong withdrew his life savings of £27,000 and set fire to it in the street, to show his disgust at the bank's low interest rates. Police managed to stop 64-year-old Chan Pak-yu after he had destroyed a total of £1,600.
Issue 418: July 19th 2003

A German motorist collided with a truck after being temporarily blinded by a pair of flying underpants. The knickers were tossed out of a van and flew through the window of a Volkswagen Passat going in the opposite direction, temporarily blinding the driver. Police believe the van was full of naked men.
Issue 420: August 2nd 2003

A family from Ohio discovered a tramp in their attic, 18 months after he secretly moved in. June and Robert Curlew unearthed the intruder while investigating a nasty smell. The elderly man, who has not been identified, had broken into their house while they were away and set up home in the attic, with a pile of blankets and a stack of canned food stolen from their kitchen. He was using an empty coffee pot as a makeshift lavatory, causing the odour which led to his detection.
Issue 422: August 16th 2003

A South African woman tried to sue her bosses after finding a cooked penis in a canteen stew. Hospital cleaner Sophie Matlala, 60, was tucking into her goulash when she found a lump of meat which she couldn't cut or chew. After a close inspection together with her work mates, the group agreed it was a penis. Matlala, who was violently sick and had to have psychiatric help, tried to claim £210,000 but a court in Pretoria dismissed her case. She has since become a vegetarian.
Issue 422: August 16th 2003

Staff at a computer software firm in Germany are claiming unfair dismissal after a mailroom supervisor spiked their drinks with laxative and then sacked them for spending too long in the lavatory. Helmut Kruger was caught on a hidden camera pouring a sachet of laxative into a coffee pot, and then telling an employee that he had just brewed a fresh pot "that has your name written all over it". He also removed the paper from the stalls, so that embarrassed staff had to shout for help.
Issue 423: August 23rd 2003

A Texan surgeon who left his watch inside a patient during a gallbladder operation is demanding that she pays him back for it. The watch was discovered after Harrie Reinski returned to the hospital complaining of post-surgical pain. Her surgeon, Franklin Gifling, apparently took one look at the X-ray and shouted: "Hey, I've been looking all over for this!" Now he wants her to reimburse him for the $21,000 timepiece. "No one can expect me to wear a watch that's been sloshing about inside a person's body for weeks," he says.

Issue 427: Sept 20th 2003

A woman from Cheltenham who had her debit card stolen was delighted when £291.40 was deposited in her account a few days later. The thief had used Jacqueline Boanson's card to place two £50 bets at Ladbrokes, and his chosen horses romped home first. Unfortunately for him, the bookmakers paid the winnings directly into Mrs Boanson's bank account.

Issue 429: Oct 4th 2003

A dancer who specialises in putting out candles with her bottom is suing a nightclub for damages. Kirsten McDermott, who weighs 13 stone, was snuffing out the candles on a birthday cake at Heaven, in London, when the table she was standing on collapsed. Now she is demanding £20,000 in compensation for a broken leg.

Issue 430: Oct 11th 2003

A novelty toy dog which farts when it bends over sparked a major security alert at a US airport. Dave Rogerson, from Leeds, was amazed when his mechanical terrier set off an explosives detector at Norfolk airport, Virginia. Traced of the explosive TNT were found in its "wind-breaking" mechanism, and armed security guards sprang into action. Mr Rogerson, 31, was grilled by FBI agents, who took swabs from the toy's rear end before allowing them both to proceed with their journey.

Issue 433: Nov 1st 2003

Thousands of Japanese tourists have had their holidays blighted by a Japanese-English phrase book containing deliberately misleading translations. One man from Okinawa, who lost his way in America, was chased for five blocks after he asked a stranger, "I know martial arts. May I kiss your ass?" instead of, "I am lost. Which way is uptown?" The bogus dictionary, 50,000 copies of which were sold in Japan before it was withdrawn, is thought to be the work of a disgruntled Japanese tourism official.

Issue 435: Nov 15th 2003

The winner of the "world's biggest liar" competition has been accused of cheating. Abrie Kruger, 24, from South Africa, is the first foreign winner of the Cumbrian contest, in which a panel of judges choose the most credible tall tale. But Kruger's yarn – about how he was crowned King of the Wasdale Valley – was denounced by former winner John Graham, who claims Kruger broke the rules by reading from a script and using props.
Issue 438: Dec 6th 2003

A Missouri police officer was fired after he guzzled 70 beers that had been confiscated from underage drinkers. The officer is suing to get his job back, arguing that he simply followed orders to dispose of the beer. "Turning beer into urine is disposal," says his lawyer.
Issue 440: Dec 20th 2003

A glue-sniffer who broke into a glue factory looking for the ultimate high was discovered stuck to the floor. Bill Henderson broke into the Durable Fit glue factory in Sydney and made a beeline for the blending room to inhale the fumes. But he knocked over a 500-gallon vat of contact cement, slipped and got stuck to the ground. Workers who found him 12 hours later had to prise him free with shovels. "He was screaming and hollering," said glue-viscosity tester Florence Mabely. "I kept telling him to shut up or I'd super-glue his mouth."
Issue 442: Jan 10th 2004

Italian police are looking for a woman with huge breasts who has gone on the run after failing to pay for her implants. The 46-year-old woman, who has not been named, disappeared from a clinic in Rome shortly after the £5,000 operation. "This has happened to me several times before," said surgeon Dr Salhi. "Last December a man had a penis enlargement and disappeared without paying."
Issue 449: Feb 28th 2004

An Ohio woman found an unexpected garnish in her salad at a local burger joint. She tried to chew it, thinking it was a bean, before spitting it out. It turned out to be a thumb tip from a worker who had cut himself chopping the salad the night before. "Physically, I think she's OK," said Health Commissioner William Franks – "other than hysteria."
Issue 452: March 20th 2004

A boat carrying 60 tourists on Lake Travis, Texas, capsized after all the passengers rushed to one side to look at nude bathers. The double-decker barge had moored alongside Hippie Hollow nudist beach during Splash Day – a naked festival for gays and lesbians. As the passengers rushed to gawp, the boat tipped over and sank. Naked revellers dived in to rescue the tourists, all of whom made it safely ashore.
Issue 459: May 8th 2004

America's top competitive eater, Crazy Legs Conti, has been defeated by a box of popcorn. At the New York premiere of Zen and the Art of Competitive Eating – a film based on Conti's life – the 33-year-old lowered himself into a "popcorn sarcophagus", vowing to munch his way out. The 50 cubic feet of salted popcorn proved too much, however, and he gave up halfway through.
Issue 461: May 22nd 2004

A Munich bus driver called Slobodan Milosevic has had his post office account frozen because officials think he is the former Yugoslav president. "I tried to explain that in Serbia my name is as common as Hans Schmidt here, but they told me Hans Schmidt was not a war criminal," says Mr Milosevic, who moved to Germany 32 years ago. The Muenchner Postbank have given him a week to prove he is not the former dictator before his savings are seized for war reparations.
Issue 464: June 6th 2004

A hospital in Agartala, India, is under investigation after staff were caught using the morgue to store fish for market traders. Hilsa fish, a local delicacy, have been stored among the corpses since March last year.
Issue 467: July 3rd 2004

A car crashed into Gordon White's living room last week – exactly a year after the same car, driven by the same driver, crashed into the same room. Eric Williams, 60, is believed to have suffered a blackout both times, leaving the road at the same spot in Cleckheaton, West Yorkshire. It took White nine weeks to clear up the mess last time, and a full year to redecorate. "I've only just finished getting the house how I want it," he said. "If I'd known this would happen, I would have used cheaper wallpaper."
Issue 469: July 17th 2004

Two policemen have been suspended after allegedly joining in with a porn shoot. The two officers, aged 30 and 34, had been called to calm a crowd which had spotted a porn film being made in Soho, London. But the officers talked their way into the crew's van, where they were secretly filmed letting the women play with their handcuffs, dress up in their uniforms and perform sex acts on them. The company behind the film, Twin Cheeks II, is now threatening to post the film on the internet. "It was unbelievable," says the director, Marino Franchi. "They just decided to have their very own private porn movie while on the job."
Issue 474: August 21st 2004

A Japanese man burnt his parents' house down while trying to kill a mosquito. Tatsuo Onishi was relaxing outside the family home in Matsuyama when the mosquito began to annoy him. The 22-year-old chased the bug around the house squirting insecticide at it. When that failed, he lit a cigarette to calm his nerves. The insecticide caught fire and the house exploded into flames. The mosquito was killed in the blaze.
Issue 476: Sept 4th 2004

A Peterborough resident was shocked to find a trail of blood leading from her front door and part of her post-man's finger inside the letter box. Katrina Salmon, 38, also found a note pinned to the door: "Please excuse the blood. Our postman got his finger caught in your letter box and could not retrieve the remainder. Please call us." Mrs Salmon located the digit – which belonged to a teenage worker – but could not face storing it in the freezer to be reattached, so she threw it away.
Issue 479: Sept 25th 2004

A woman who got confused by the signposting at an Idaho airport ended up driving through the terminal building. The senior citizen was trying to drop her rental car off at Boise Airport, but followed the wrong signs. She drove the car through a set of automatic doors, into the terminal and past the baggage reclaim area, before stopping outside the rental-car counter. There was no damage to the building, no one was hurt and she hasn't been prosecuted.
Issue 482: Oct 16th 2004

A German woman caused £15,000 of damage after trying to make her breakfast at the wheel of her car. Julia Bauer, 21, from Bochum, laid out a bowl, a packet of muesli, a pint of milk and a spoon on the passenger seat, before heading off for work. En route to the office, she managed to pour the cereal, but lost control of the vehicle while leaning over to steady the bowl.
Issue 486: Nov 13th 2004

A group of students staying at a friend's house committed the ultimate social faux pas when they drank the remains of their host's grandfather. Returning to Jakub Havlat's cottage after a night on the sauce, the Czechs decided to have a sobering cup of coffee. It was only when Jakub came home that they realised the grains in the tin were not Nescafé, but ashes. "It was barely drinkable but we needed to sober up so we just downed it," said one of the students. "When we discovered our mistake, we sobered up immediately."
Issue 488: Nov 27th 2004

A 78-year-old Chinese granny scaled the wall of her apartment block after getting locked out of her fifth floor flat. Nie Sanmie ignored the pleas of her neighbours in Changsha, Hunan province, and started climbing, using window grilles as footholds. Only when she got stuck below an air-conditioning unit on the fourth floor did she allow her neighbours to call the emergency services. "I must have been drunk," she admitted afterwards. "I hope others don't follow my example and risk their lives."
Issue 497: Feb 5th 2005

A judge in Oklahoma is being investigated for allegedly using a pneumatic penis pump in court. Clerks in Judge Donald Thompson's courtroom reported hearing a rhythmic "whooshing" sound coming from behind the bench, and said the judge often seemed distracted. One clerk photographed the pump on Thompson's chair when he went out for lunch. Thompson, 58, insists it was a joke gift from a friend, and says he never used it while the court was in session.
Issue 500: Feb 26th 2005

Even illegal immigrants can feel too invisible in New York. Ming Kuang Chen, 33, got stuck in a lift last week while delivering a takeaway to the Bronx – and stayed there without food or water for three days. Chen pressed the button for assistance, but only knew enough English to shout: "No good! No good!" The caretaker assumed he was drunk. When he was eventually found, Chen refused to stay in hospital and disappeared back into anonymity.
Issue 507: April 16th 2005

The world's first laughter school has opened in Berlin. Susanne Maier started the school after a survey revealed that Germans only laugh for six minutes a day (compared with 19 minutes for Italians). She gets her pupils to stand in groups, chortling in different ways. "I am hoping to see laughter schools opening up every-where," she says. "Germany will become a land of laughter – and Berlin the laughter capital of Europe."
Issue 518: July 2nd 2005

A lorry-driver in Germany drove two miles down a motorway with a Smart car wedged under his bumper. Klaus Buergermeister, 53, said he felt a slight bump when he turned onto the A1 at Leverkusen, but took it for a stone on the road. The terrified driver of the Smart car only escaped when the lorry was pulled over by police. "I couldn't believe it," said Buergermeister. "I got out of the truck and saw there was a car stuck on the front."
Issue 512: May 21st 2005

A teenager in New Zealand who tried to rob an industrial container was buried by an avalanche of peas. The 17-year-old used a cigarette lighter to melt the plastic ties securing the shipping container, but as soon as he opened the door, he was engulfed up to his neck in peas. Police used a fork-lift truck to dig him out, and he was fined £77 in damages – half the price of the peas.
Issue 512: May 21st 2005

A man who passed out drunk on a railway line in Dmitrievka, Russia, kept on sleeping while a 140-tonne train roared over his prone body. "I saw a man lying between the tracks and tried to stop, but it was too late," said train driver Vladimir Slabiy. "When I got out and looked he was still there, fast asleep. It was lucky he was so drunk. If he had woken from the noise and lifted his head, that would have been the end of him."
Issue 529: Sept 17th 2005

An Australian man wearing a woollen shirt and a nylon jacket generated so much static electricity that he set a carpet on fire. When cleaner Frank Clewer walked into an office building in Warrnambool, Australia, he was unaware of the electrical current accumulating as his clothes rubbed together. But then there was a loud popping sound and the carpet burst into flames. After evacuating the building, fire officials confiscated Clewer's jacket. "We tested his clothes with a static electricity field meter and measured a current of 40,000 volts," said fire official Henry Barton. "Which is one step shy of spontaneous combustion."
Issue 531: Oct 1st 2005

An artist who chained his legs together so he could sketch them had to hop for 12 hours through the desert after losing the key. Trevor Corneliusien, 26, wrapped the chain around his ankles while camping in California. "He had to hop through boulders and sand," said deputy sheriff Ryan Ford. "He brought the drawing with him. It was a pretty good depiction of how a chain would look wrapped round your legs."
Issue 545: Jan 14th 2006

Stranger Than Fiction

"I spent ages preparing for this show but it looks like I'm going to have to buy a dictionary to win it," said Charlotte Anderson, one of four girls who tied as Miss Cardiff only to be told that the bone who writes the best 100 words essay on "Why I Want To Be Miss Cardiff" will go forwards for the Miss World Competition.
Issue 11: August 5th 1995

A Tokyo hotel has installed sound effects in its phone booth so cheating husbands can pretend they're stuck at a railway station.
Issue 24: Nov 4th 1995

Entrepreneurs in Singapore are cashing in on Nick Leeson's trial for fraud by selling a calculator which gets its maths wrong.
Issue 29: Dec 9th 1995

Keebler Cookies, an American biscuit company, will not allow its mascot to be used in a play opening in Chicago called 'Vampire Lesbians of Sodom'. "Our elf cannot be associated with any production which has 'lesbian' in the title," said a spokesman.
Issue 30: Dec 16th 1995

A Swedish couple who named their son "Brfxxccxxmnpckcc-111mm nprxvclmnckssqlbb-11116 " were told by tax authorities to find a shorter name. They chose "A".
Issue 119: Sept 13th 1997

A New York art exhibition featuring 500 slugs slithering over women's dirty knickers – by conceptual artist Vladimir Burschwanger – was ruined when a cleaner poured salt on the slugs to kill them and took the underwear home to wash. "I am not upset," said Burschwanger. "Art is a story, and this one just had an unhappy ending."
Issue 128: Nov 15th 1997

TV presenter John Henson was so desperate to get Dustin Hoffman on his chat show that he went on a nine-day hunger strike until the actor agreed to appear. But by the time Hoffman got to the studio, Henson was so weak he had to be wheeled off to hospital. "For me to work with Dustin on a crappy little cable telly show is the ultimate," said Henson. When the interview took place, Henson was still attached to a food drip.
Issue 144: March 14th 1998

A phantom streaker has been terrifying motorists by running along a busy motorway with his underpants on his head. The man has been making his regular 400-yard nude dashes along the hard shoulder of the M11 for two years. Despite having been seen by hundreds of people he has never been caught. "You know what Cambridge is like. Nothing surprises me these days," said investigating officer PC Plant.
Issue 147: April 14th 1998

Albert Matanle, a 3ft 6in Ghanaian midget, was caned by the headmaster of a school he did not even attend. Matanle, 45, a blackboard salesman, visited the school in Accra to drum up business. When he was shown into the headmaster's study he was mistaken for a pupil and given six of the best for not wearing a uniform. Despite his pleas, he was then made to stand in the corner for three hours. He is suing the school for assault.
Issue 164: August 1st 1998

A French clown called Booboo was stabbed when a schoolteacher mistook him for a sexual deviant. He was visiting the Caneuil Infants School in Cahors, when he got trapped in the lavatory. After yelling for help he decided to climb out of the window. But he was obliged to remove his padded trousers to squeeze through. As he emerged feet-first in his boxer shorts, the teacher stabbed him in the buttock with a knitting needle while screaming "Pervert!" "I saw a half-naked man in giant shoes climbing through the window of a children's toilet," she said. "What was I supposed to think?"
Issue 173: Oct 3rd 1998

Officials in Pori, Finland, are making litter louts stand all day where they were caught dropping litter and chant: "I am filthy", while wearing plastic pig snouts and ears.
Issue 180: Nov 28th 1998

Charles Fay, 43, who has had a remote control fitted in his penis to cure impotence, gets an erection every time his neighbours in Houston, Texas, use their electronic garage doors. He is suing the hospital.
Issue 185: Jan 2nd 1999

An angry woman from Bishop Auckland, Co. Durham, dialled 999 on New Year's Eve to complain that her pizza had the wrong topping. Moments later, another woman rang to say that her budgie had fallen off its perch, and a third called to ask police to bring her a pair of tights to replace the ones she had laddered.
Issue 186: Jan 9th 1999

Brian Doran, aged 2, is addicted to plasterboard, and has already ruined three rooms in his house in Redhill, Surrey, by munching through it. His mother Donna, 30, said: "He won't eat ordinary food unless I pretend to sprinkle plasterboard over the top."
Issue 191: Feb 13th 1999

In response to Nostradamus's prediction that a calamity will strike in July, a Japanese lingerie firm is selling a bra with a sensor that alerts its wearer to incoming missiles. The Armageddon Bra, made by Triumph, includes a sensor on the shoulder strap to warn of objects falling from the sky. For more efficient operation, it should be worn without outer garments.
Issue 205: May 22nd 1999

When Deborah Wilkins found that her pet fish had grown too big for their tank, she ate them. The first to go was a black shark. Then she barbecued an Amazonian pacu, which had grown to two-and-a-half feet, having been imported as a two-inch baby. It was served up to guests with a tangy sauce. "It's wrong," she admitted. "But it was getting far too big. And by eating it, we completed the circle of life. Now, hopefully, its spirit has gone back to the Amazon."
Issue 211: July 3rd 1999

A former Naval commander has revealed how a British warship was attacked by the Loch Ness Monster during World War II. In 1944, Vivian Owers was with a flotilla practising beach landings in Loch Ness in preparation for the D-day landings. Sailing down a clear stretch of water, one of the ships was attacked and left with missing propeller blades. "There were no logs in the water and our only explanation was that it must have been the monster," he told the Daily Star. Owers, 77, had never spoken of the incident because he feared it was a military secret.
Issue 219: August 28th 1999

Lee Armstrong, 28, has started a cleaning service for dolls' houses in Chelmsford, Essex. He says that children are too busy playing computer games to do it themselves.
Issue 220: Sept 4th 1999

An Australian model cheated death when a bullet bounced off her breast implant, reports The Sun. Jayne Pikering, 27, who was shot during a brawl in a Sydney nightclub, was flung across the room when the .45 calibre bullet tore through her left breast. The rubbery gel implant deflected the bullet, stopping it from becoming embedded in vital organs. "Police told me that type of bullet goes right through bullet-proof vests," said Jayne. "I believe if it wasn't for my implants I wouldn't be here now."
Issue 232: Nov 27th 1999

Peter Bakel, a surgeon in Rotterdam, has been sacked from Evanglishe Community Hospital for chain-smoking during a triple-bypass operation. "The floor was littered with butts," said Nurse Bettie Serphos. "He smoked those cigarettes down to the nub, through his surgical mask – then reached over for a clamp and dropped ash into the patient's incision." Bakel was unrepentant: "I operate better when I smoke," he said. "I was at least three feet away from the oxygen tanks."
Issue 234: Dec 11th 1999

Natives of an isolated village in Zaire have taken a helicopter hostage, believing it to be a giant bird. When John Barr was forced to land his ailing chopper near the village, the locals swarmed all over it and took Barr prisoner. The tribe, who have been shoving bowls of food and water into the cockpit, have demanded $100,000 from Zaire Air Charter as ransom. They say they will kill the helicopter if their demands are not met.
Issue 241: Feb 5th 2000

Pizza deliveryman Casey Fine, from Sydney, Australia, refused to go to hospital after being shot in the head by muggers last week. Fine – who had a hole in his cheek and a bullet lodged in his skull – insisted on delivering his pizza before seeing a doctor. "I saw the pizza on the seat, knew there were people counting on it, and delivered it so it wouldn't get cold. The customers wanted their food, not some lame excuse," he explained.

Issue 248: March 25th 2000

Brendan San, a 21-year-old student, has been short-listed for an international art prize in Norwich. His work consists of two cheques, each for £1,000, made out to the two judges.

Issue 252: April 22nd 2000

A study in Chicago has revealed that people with large bottoms are cleverer than those with small bottoms. On average, large-bottomed people have an IQ 29 points higher.

Issue 256: May 20th 2000

Sharon Webb, 47, of Glastonbury, Somerset, is so terrified of reversing her car she has spent 25 years only driving forward.

Issue 257: May 27th 2000

John Evans, 51, of Marlpool, Derbyshire, has claimed a world record by balancing 92 people on his head in one hour at Lowestoft, Suffolk.

Issue 267: August 5th 2000

Unholy goings on have been reported at Singalonga Sound of Music, the karaoke version of the musical which is playing at cinemas around the country. The shows are attended by Julie Andrews fans, who dress up as characters in the film and sing along with their heroine. But it appears that the accompanying 'nun lookalike' competition has been infiltrated by real nuns, who have been sneaking in and carrying off all the top prizes. "Undercover nuns can be a real problem," said producer Lisle Turner. "They don't get out much so when they do escape they tend to get a little out of control."

Issue 270: August 26th 2000

A US radio station is offering its listeners the opportunity to win plastic surgery to transform themselves into Britney Spears. WAKS FM in Ohio is promising their winner £2,700 worth of liposuction, tummy tucks and breast surgery to resemble the pop star. Entrants have to write an essay on why they deserve to go under the knife.

Issue 274: Sep 23rd 2000

The number of Elvis Presley impersonators is spiralling out of control. American research has identified 85,000 Elvis impersonators compared with just 150 in 1977, the year he died. If growth continues at the same rate, one third of the world will be impersonating Elvis by the year 2019.
Issue 285: Dec 9th 2000

A first-aid book issued to Australian factory workers includes the advice: "Shake the victim and shout, 'Are you alright?'"
Issue 285: Dec 9th 2000

A pensioner in Hokkaido, Japan, was choking on sticky rice when his daughter rushed to the rescue with her vacuum cleaner. The woman wrenched out her spluttering father's false teeth, stuffed the nozzle into his mouth and turned the suction power to "high". "A vacuum cleaner can be useful in an emergency," said rescue official Toshiyuki Matsuura, "but I wouldn't recommend it to everyone."
Issue 289: Jan 13th 2001

The TUC is starting a telephone helpline for people who work at telephone helpline centres so that they can complain about conditions at work.
Issue 291: Jan 27th 2001

A Brazilian woman has pledged to fight "human mediocrity" by t urning herself into a cow. Priscilla Davanzo, 22, has visited a tattoo parlour three times a week for nine months to be covered in black and white patches. "What I am trying to say to people is that I want to be a cow," she says. "Cows are the only animals which can digest the same food twice. That's something that human beings, who consider themselves so superior, are unable to do."
Issue 291: Jan 27th 2001

An underfunded TV station in Moscow has a new hit show called Who Wants to be Fabulously Wealthy, with a top prize of £32.60.
Issue 296: March 3rd 2001

The world's most tasteless theme park has opened in Lithuania. Visitors to Stalin World – dedicated to the prison camps of the former Soviet Union – will wander around under the gaze of mannequins with fake machine guns in watchtowers. The cafe serves gruel, and there are plants to re-enact the torture of labour camp victims.
Issue 296: March 3rd 2001

A Russian engineer has invented a talking vodka bottle. Every time the top is removed, the bottle suggests another round of drinks. As more vodka is drunk, the bottle gets bawdier. Eventually, it sings saucy drinking songs, burps and laughs uproariously.
Issue 297: March 10th 2001

When Walter Comber cut a hole in the ceiling of his home in Torquay, Devon, 200 old £5 notes fell on his head, wrapped in the horoscope page of a 1955 newspaper. His star sign read: "A happy day ahead."
Issue 298: March 17th 2001

Admiral Sir Alan West, Commander-in-Chief Fleet, was briefing troops in the wardroom of HMS Lancaster during a tour of the Gulf when he was interrupted by someone shouting "arse" and "bollocks" in a high-pitched voice. The abuse, it transpired, was coming from a cupboard where the troops had hidden their foul-mouthed mascot, an African grey parrot called Sunny. "Everything was going okay," said one officer, "until the word 'arse' came from the cupboard. Sir Alan looked a little stunned, but just carried on as normal. God knows what he was thinking." Sunny has also been trained to recite Michael Caine's famous line, "Zulus, thousands of 'em", and whistle the theme tune from The Great Escape.
Issue 313: June 30th 2001

A Texas travel agency is arranging the world's first nude flight. Castaways Travel, which specialises in holidays for nudists, has chartered a Boeing 727 for a 3 May flight from Miami to Cancun. Passengers will be fully dressed for check-in and take-off, but will be allowed to strip once the plane reaches cruising altitude. "This is not a Mile High club," said a spokesman. "Many travellers just prefer to fly in the nude."
Issue 394: Feb 1st 2003

A vintage Chevrolet bought at an auction in Hamburg, Germany, turned out to be a real bargain. When the new owner started tinkering about with the car – which had been impounded by customs when it arrived from Mexico six years ago – he discovered £300,000 worth of cocaine concealed inside.
Issue 418: July 19th 2003

An inflatable snowman has been sending its owner post-cards from exotic locations around the world. The 5ft snowman, who signs his name Frosty, was stolen from Helen Bevan's garden in Wales last year. She has since received cards from Tenerife, Antigua, Thailand, Mexico, Malaysia and Hong Kong. "At first I thought it was funny, with Frosty complaining about the heat and telling tales of his travels," says Bevan."But I have no idea who the joker is."
Issue 428: Sept 27th 2003

Stressed managers in Austria can ring a mobile phone to listen to "the genuine woodland sound of silence". The phones have been distributed around forests in Austria, so that callers can experience the quietness of nature. The Call Wood project has proved such a popular stress-buster that Call Waterfall and Call Mountain Top lines are now being planned.
Issue 445: Jan 31st 2004

A Dallas company is making £2m a year selling demotivational products to pessimists. Despair Inc's most popular products include a mug with a line which shows when it is half empty, and Bittersweets – flavoured lovehearts for the dysfunctional and dejected, featuring messages such as "Table for 1" or "Peaked at 17". The catalogue (at www.despair.com) also features a fashion range – Despairwear – which includes a T-shirt with the slogan: "Unleash the power of mediocrity". "A lot of people find motivational products demeaning," says founder E.L. Kersten. "We are the brand for cynics, pessimists and the chronically unsuccessful."
Issue 446: Feb 7th 2004

Children should be allowed to pick their nose and eat it, says a leading Austrian doctor. "With the finger you can get to places you just can't reach with a handkerchief, keeping your nose far cleaner," says Dr Friedrich Bischinger. "And eating the dry remains of what you pull out is a great way of strengthening the body's immune system." Ingesting the bacteria from your nose helps inoculate the body against illness, which may be why this instinctual behaviour evolved. "I recommend a new approach, where children are encouraged to pick their nose."
Issue 455: April 10th 2004

Two Bosnian brothers who can drink as much as they want without getting drunk have discovered why: they each have a spare set of fully functioning kidneys. Josip Galic, 69, from Kucetine, found out about the extra kidneys after he had a car accident. His brother, Ante, discovered his after a routine-check up. "At least it explains why I could drink all my friends under the table and never have a hangover," said Josip, who says he isn't planning to sell his spare kidneys. "I'd give them for free if family members or close friends needed them."
Issue 449: Feb 28th 2004

A nine-piece orchestra gave a concert with a difference in Hamburg last week, playing 90lb of specially-carved vegetables. The Viennese Vegetable Orchestra performed a selection of classics using instruments such as a flute made from a carrot, a saxophone carved out of a cucumber and a violin made of leeks.
Issue 463: June 5th 2004

A German inventor stands to make a fortune after devising a gadget to stop men missing the lavatory when they pee. The WC Ghost, which fits into the bowl, springs into action every time the lavatory seat is raised. A bossy woman's voice shouts: "What are you up to? Put the seat back down right away. You are definitely not to pee standing up. You will make a mess." Inventor Alex Benkhardt has already sold 1.6 million of the gadgets in Germany, and is currently in negotiations to market the device in Britain.
Issue 463: June 5th 2004

Dudley dustman Tim Byrne is so dedicated to his job that he never stops – even on holiday. Each summer, he picks a resort, then fixes up shifts with the local waste-disposal firm. "Rubbish is such a big part of my life that I never want to switch off," says Byrne, who has emptied bins everywhere from Cornwall to Kefalonia. "Other people look forward to a dip in the pool, but I can't wait to go out on the rounds with the lads."
Issue 493: Jan 8th 2005

Fishermen in the Caspian Sea claim to have spotted a merman. The marine humanoid is described as 5ft 6in long, with webbed hands and black-green hair. "The creature was swimming a parallel course near the boat for a long time," said Gafar Gasanof, captain of an Azeri trawler. "At first we thought it was a big fish, but then we spotted hair on the head of the monster."
Issue 510: May 7th 2005

Woolworths is to increase the size of its "Hot Lips" sweeties to reflect the fashion for collagen implants. The chain store – Britain's biggest sweet seller – decided to make the changes after customers complained that the Hot Lips seemed a bit thin. "Celebrities have changed our customers' perceptions of size," said Pick'n'Mix buyer Jennifer Salamony.
Issue 516: June 18th 2005

A Burmese woman has spontaneously changed gender. Thin Sandar, 21, a chicken-seller from Rangoon, said she always dreamed of being a man, but was still surprised last month to find herself growing a penis. "On the morning of the full moon day of 21 June, I noticed my thing was not the same as before, and my breasts disappeared," she said. "So I called out and showed it all to my mum and dad. It was very strange." Sandar's new gender will allow her to pursue another dream – to become a Buddhist monk.

Issue 522: July 30th 2005

Since the introduction of The Freedom of Information Act, the Ministry of Defence has received around 300 enquiries a month – not all of which are easy to answer. "There are thousands of questions I could 7ask but what I really want to know is are there extra terrestrials on this planet?" wrote one little girl. "Please, please, please could you tell me if there are photos? Because I really need to know. I PROMISE to keep it a secret."

Issue 525: August 20th 2005

The world's first lavatory-cleaning college is to open in Singapore next month. The centre will show lavatory cleaners how to hone their hygiene skills, as well as offering modules in associated crafts such as changing light bulbs, repairing leaky taps and removing urine salt from under the rim.

Issue 528: Sept 8th 2005

A plastic doll of a middle-aged librarian from Seattle has become America's fastest-selling action toy. The five-inch figurine – whose only action is raising a finger to her lips to request silence – is modelled on librarian Nancy Pearl, 60, who jokingly suggested to a toy maker at a dinner party in 2002 that her profession needed a public hero. Some 100,000 Librarian Action Dolls have since been sold, overtaking sales of Buffy the Vampire Slayer dolls.

Issue 530: Sept 24th 2005

The hottest accessory at London fashion week was a clip-on smile, modelled on the Hollywood star of your choice. "A dentist called Jeff Golub-Evans came up with the idea of creating these snap-in veneers which can be placed over patients' teeth, allowing them to look like their favourite celebrity," says an insider. "So far the most popular requests are for Julia Roberts's teeth."

Issue 531: Oct 1st 2005

A blind woman has baffled scientists in Germany by learning to distinguish colours by touch. "This ability really gives me more independence," said Gabriele Simon, 48. "I don't need to ask my mother what to wear anymore."
Issue 534: Oct 22nd 2005

Researchers in Sweden have discovered that exposure to art can ease constipation. Tests on 20 elderly women, who met regularly to discuss art for four months, showed a wide range of physical benefits, including more regular bowel movements. "Their attitudes became more positive," says researcher Britt-Maj Wikstrom. "Their blood pressure went in the right direction and they used fewer laxatives."
Issue 535: Oct 29th 2005

An American weatherman has accused Japanese gangsters of creating Hurricane Katrina as vengeance for Hiroshima. Scott Stevens, a forecaster for an Idaho TV channel, claims that the Japanese villains used a secret electro-magnetic generator to create the hurricane. "Our weather," he says, "has been stolen from us."
Issue 536: Nov 5th 2005

This year's must-have Christmas present for American children is a £40,000 wendy house, with electricity, plumbing and a flat-screen TV. The custom-made houses – designed by architects to raise money for a homeless charity – are 8ft wide and 10ft high, with features including hand-carved oak staircases, fitted carpets, slate roofs and a garage to park a toy car in. "They are mini-mansions," says a spokesman for the Project Playhouse charity. "Any child would have their dream come true with a playhouse like this."
Issue 541: Dec 10th 2005

What's In A Name

When Mr Heron reported that he had run over a peacock, police at Kingsbridge, Devon, sent PC Partridge to investigate.
Issue 121: Sept 21st 1997

Thatcher and Heath, two fraudsters from Henley-on-Thames, were jailed for four years and 18 months last week. The judged who sentenced them at Oxford Crown Court was called Harold Wilson.
Issue 116: August 23rd 1997

A £1 million French lottery prize has been won by Mr and Mrs Lotterie of Bordeaux. John-Paul Lotterie, 65, said: "We knew our numbers would come up eventually."
Issue 132: Dec 13th 1997

Marci Klein, daughter of Calvin Klein, says there is a downside to having a famous designer as a father: "Every time I'm about to go to bed with a guy I see my Dad's name all over his underwear. It is very off-putting."
Issue 133: Dec 20th 1997

A judge in Georgia, USA, dismissed a court case against John Fairytale, saying that anyone with a name like that had been punished enough already.
Issue 153: May 16th 1998

The world's first Practical Jokers Conference in Germany had to be closed down by local authorities because it became too raucous. The event was plagued by problems from the start. The conference hall had to be repeatedly evacuated because of false bomb scares, three Swedish delegates were hospitalised after sitting on electrified lavatories and the first-night party was ruined when someone spiked the punch with laxative. The final straw came when a US delegate had a fatal coronary after finding a fake cockroach in his sauerkraut.
Issue 160: July 4th 1998

Rivals in a beauty contest had to be separated by police after they started punching each other when the result was announced.
The battered girls in Orlando, Florida, had been competing for the title of Miss Sweetness.
Issue 160: July 4th 1998

A convention is to be held in Austria this month to discuss the problem of embarrassing names. Among those attending will be Adolf Hitler and Heinrich Himmler.
Issue 169: Sept 5th 1998

Roberto Castinelli, 29, from Lake Michigan, has resigned from Oakside Infants School after fellow teachers refused to address him by his new name, which he changed by deed poll. While Castinelli's bank had no problem issuing cheque books made out to "Strawberry Funkin 'O Punkin' the Gay Prince of Hell", concerned parents removed their children from his classes in protest. "There were too many unfortunate incidents at PTA meetings," said the deputy principal.
Issue 188: Jan 23rd 1999

A convicted robber is to get a retrial in Alabama under the pseudonym Mr X. The judge ruled that the jury had been prejudiced by his real name, Robin Banks.
Issue 196: March 20th 1999

In Leeds, 30-year-old Michael Howard changed his name by deed poll to Yorkshire Bank Plc Are Fascist Bastards when they charged him £20 for a £10 overdraft. He then demanded to have his 69p balance repaid by cheque, made out in his new name.
Issue 198: April 3rd 1999

Sergeant Rabbits, a wildlife officer for Devon police, has recently been promoted from a PC. His fellow wildlife officers are PC Crowe and Sergeant Hunter.
Issue 220: Sept 4th 1999

Heinrich K of Frankfurt has been given a 10-month suspended sentence and fined £680 for assaulting a traffic cop. "Here's something for your mouth," shouted Heinrich, as he punched the policeman in the face after the cop refused to remove the ticket from his illegally parked car. Heinrich is an anger-management consultant.
Issue 229: Nov 6th 1999

An anonymous policeman fooled the Ordnance Survey into including Letsby Avenue on a new street map. He used headed South Yorkshire Police notepaper to suggest the name for a new road outside a Sheffield police station. Letsby Avenue, the only street of that name in the country, has now been officially adopted.
Issue 243: Feb 19th 2000

Nicki Nutting, 28, became Mrs Nutting-Toulouse when she wed Robert Toulouse in Birmingham last week.
Issue 265: July 22nd 2000

One of Bristol's best-loved police officers patrols the city on a 15mph battery-powered bicycle. His name is PC Duke Hazard.
Issue 280: Nov 4th 2000

Dr John Looney, a child psychiatrist from North Carolina, heads a list of aptly named doctors drawn up by The Seattle Times. The paper also discovered a stomach specialist called Harvey Guttman, a Dr Killman, Dr Butcher, Dr Surgeon, Dr Postumus and a dozen doctors called Slaughter.
Issue 300: March 31st 2001

A 24-year-old Californian named Truly Gold has married a man called Cary S. Boring, to become Mrs Truly Boring. "I'm not really boring," she insisted. "I can be the life of the party."
Issue 301: April 7th 2001

The signpost to the Aberdeenshire village of Lost has been stolen.
Issue 320: August 18th 2001

For this year's Martin Luther King Day, the Florida town of Lauderhill paid tribute to black actor James Earl Jones. But the ceremony went horribly wrong when the commemorative plaque was unveiled, reading: "Thank you James Earl Ray for keeping the dream alive. " Ray was convicted of murdering King in 1968.
Issue 342: Jan 26th 2002

A public meeting organised by Bath and Northeast Somerset council was not a success. Just one member of the public turned up. The subject was Voter Apathy.
Issue 348: March 9th 2002

An American man called Jack Ass is suing the makers of MTV's stunt comedy show Jackass for giving him a bad name. Mr Ass, who changed his name from Bob Craft in 1997, wants £7m in damages "for injury to my reputation and defamation of my character which I have worked so hard to create".
Issue 391: Jan 11th 2003

A man who was grazed on the bottom by a passing bus was mollified when he noticed its destination. Arthur Pratt, from Kent, wrote a letter congratulating the bus company on the accuracy of its advertised route: "To Orpington via Pratt's Bottom".
Issue 432: Oct 25th 2003

Albuquerque man Snaphappy Fishsuit Mokiligon has won a year-long battle to change his name to plain "Variable". An earlier ruling – that the name Variable "would be contrary to the public good" – was overruled by the New Mexico state appeal court after Snaphappy argued his rights were being violated.
Issue 494: Jan 15th 2005

Apparently you're big in Germany too...

Desperate Measures

Furious at being refused a loan, Christina Hupier, 27, stripped off, smeared her body with superglue and stuck herself to her bank manager in Lyon, France. Police charged her with damaging his Armani suit.
Issue 148: April 11th 1998

A worker sacked from a Toronto aircraft factory refused to leave quietly. The Scottish technician put on a kilt, hoisted himself up on a crane and brought the factory to a standstill for three hours playing the bagpipes. "My Scots blood made me do it," he explained.
Issue 149: April 18th 1998

A Northwest Airlines pilot has been sacked for leaving his passengers on the tarmac at Detroit airport while he went into town to get a take-away. It seems he couldn't face another in-flight meal.
Issue 235: Dec 18th 1999

Rich parents in New York are visiting expensive counsellors to find out how not to spoil their children. Typical advice is not to replace the cars they crash – not instantly, that is. "Impose a little delay between cars so they realise there are consequences for wrecking them," urged Peter Walsh, a child psychiatrist. He also suggested making them fly economy class.
Issue 261: June 24th 2000

Ben Thatcher, a two-year-old toddler from London, has developed an insatiable appetite for wood, and is eating his mother out of house and home. Ben started by tucking into his cot, and has since graduated to windowsills, cupboards and doorframes. "Household wood is not the best thing for a child to eat," says a nutritionist, "but as long as it hasn't been treated it shouldn't be a problem."
Issue 307: May 19th 2001

A British motorist lost her way during a day trip to Calais and drove 800 miles across Europe looking for somewhere to turn round. Vivienne Vanderwault-Hudson, who had been shopping for cigarettes and alcohol, headed down the motorway, crossed the Pyrenees into Spain, and didn't stop until Gibraltar. "I get very scared driving – I've been stopped twice for driving too slowly. I kept hoping there would be a gap in the road, but there wasn't. So I decided to keep going."
Issue 308: May 26th 2001

A 50-stone man from Bradford may leave his house for the first time in 25 years to visit German fans. Jack Taylor, 56, refuses to go outside because he fears ridicule. But he has become a cult figure in Germany, after giving interviews to 12 TV shows. "They say I'm a living legend there," he says. "I don't understand it."
Issue 314: July 7th 2001

The Madam Tussauds wax-work of TV gardener Alan Titchmarsh is kissed so often by female fans that staff have to clean its face every day. "If we leave him for any length of time, his cheeks start wearing away," said a spokesman for the museum.
Issue 315: July 14th 2001

A busker in Port Talbot, south Wales, has been asked to play less sentimental tunes by a nearby optician after customers got so tearful that it was impossible to test their eyes properly.
Issue 321: August 25th 2001

A pipe-fitter from South Carolina is selling his urine over the internet to people facing workplace drugs tests. Customers pay $45 for 5.5 ounces of "clean" urine in a pouch that can be strapped to the body. Kenneth Curtis claims to have sold 100,000 kits in six years.
Issue 324: Sept 15th 2001

Mother-of-two Carol Dukes made a 900-mile round trip to catch up with her 11-year-old son on a school trip because he had forgotten his GameBoy. Dukes spent £150 on planes and taxis as she dashed from her home in Berkshire to catch up with her son who was on a train to Scotland. She eventually met the train at Dumbarton and delivered the Nintendo toy. Carol, 31, said: "I know he would have been devastated to go a whole week without his GameBoy."
Issue 325: Sept 22nd 2001

A Russian conscript was so keen to get out of the army that he ate some of his bed. The frontier guard swallowed 19 metal hooks from his bunk in the hope of a medical discharge. Instead, he is to be charged with damaging state property.
Issue 328: Oct 13th 2001

A patient discharged himself from a psychiatric hospital near Aberystwyth, stole a bus to get home and then drove for ten miles picking up passengers along the way. He has since been readmitted.
Issue 328: Oct 13th 2001

A simmering row between two model-railway enthusiasts in Berlin came to a head when they agreed to divide the collection of trains they'd built up over three years. "Pierre R" (as he was called in court) laid claim to his friend Uwe's favourite locomotive, at which point Uwe stabbed him 13 times, cut off his testicles and threw him out of a ninth-storey window.
Issue 329: Oct 20th 2001

A homeless woman is suing a railway company in Santa Fe, New Mexico, for hitting her with a train. Dionne French admits she was asleep on the tracks wrapped in a brown blanket but claims that staff at the Sante Fe Southern Railway company had an obligation to see her and stop the train.
Issue 337: Dec 15th 2001

The queue to see the next Star Wars movie has begun. John Guth, 32, and Jeff Tweiten, 24, are waiting in line outside a Seattle cinema, although the film isn't due for release until March.
Issue 341: Jan 19th 2002

Staff at Karaganda zoo in Kazakhstan have been swapping endangered animals for office equipment, according to a report by government inspectors. One zoo worker gave two camels to a Ukrainian circus in exchange for a photocopier. In another deal, two Bengal tigers and a wild boar were swapped for a fax machine, a typewriter and a fridge.
Issue 346: Feb 23rd 2002

A beggar accused of making a fortune has instructed her lawyer to call a press conference denying the allegation. A Canadian newspaper claimed that Margita Bangova made more than £1,100 a week begging on the streets of Toronto. Her lawyer rebutted this, and complained that she had been forced to abandon her street corner because of the publicity.
Issue 350: March 23rd 2002

An office worker from Brighton is resorting to hypnosis in an attempt to stop him chewing ballpoint pens. John Carey's "habit" – 50 pens a week – costs him £600 a year. "It started five years ago and has spiralled out of control," he says. "My favourites are clear plastic Bic because the plastic is more chewy."
Issue 353: April 13th 2002

A 48-stone man used his stomach to save the lives of children trapped in a burning Munich orphanage. When Gunther Gerlach saw the children crying for help from the orphanage windows, he lay down on the street and invited them to jump on to his enormous belly. "He was like a human trampoline," says a witness. "The children got a few cuts and bruises, but that's better than what could have happened."
Issue 368: July 27th 2002

Elvis is set to make the ultimate comeback, says the Daily Star. A group called Americans for Cloning Elvis has in its possession eight ounces of the King's hair and a wart removed from the singer's wrist in 1958 – samples which they hope will enable scientists to create a new Elvis. "By the year 2020 we are confident that an Elvis clone will be performing live in Las Vegas," said a spokesman.
Issue 371: August 17th 2002

A frustrated London commuter startled fellow passengers when he rode on the outside of a train like Indiana Jones. Furious that he couldn't squeeze on board a crowded train at Oakleigh Park station, the mystery man hopped on to an outside ledge on the back of the train, where he clung for 20 minutes through seven miles, four stations and two tunnels before hopping off at Finsbury Park.
Issue 383: Nov 9th 2002

Indian farm labourer Mahadeb Hansda was so furious after being bitten by a cobra that he decided to exact his revenge on the deadly snake – by biting it back. Hansda tracked down the snake in a rice paddy and bit into it so fiercely that it died of its injuries. "I was in a rage," said Mahadeb, who survived his ordeal after treatment in a Calcutta hospital.
Issue 384: Nov 16th 2002

A Japanese man who choked on a ball of sticky rice was saved when his daughter sucked it out with a vacuum cleaner. The 70-year-old man was chewing a piece of mochi, a traditional rice cake, when it went down the wrong way. After failing to dislodge the food with her fingers, his daughter grabbed the Hoover, stuck the hose in his mouth and switched it on to "High". By the time paramedics arrived, the man had made a full recovery.
Issue 385: Nov 23rd 2002

An Indian man saved hundreds of lives using just his red underpants. Nimai Das was relieving himself by the train tracks near Kopai when he noticed that part of the track was broken. When he saw a train approaching, he quickly stripped off and began waving his red underpants frantically. The train driver stopped the train just in time, averting a catastrophic crash.
Issue 388: Dec 14th 2002

One of Argentina's top rock stars has told his fans he will leave the country forever unless they give him $1m. Charly Garcia – who claims he deserves the money for being famous for 20 years – has asked his fans to deposit one dollar each into a special bank account. "If that does not happen," he says, "I'll go to New York and never come back to Buenos Aires."
Issue 391: Jan 11th 2003

An American woman plans to stage a protest on behalf of those who are possessed by demons. Ms B, a 51-year-old Connecticut woman, says she is possessed by 19 demonic spirits but can't find anyone to perform an exorcism. She intends to demonstrate in front of the Norwich Diocese to draw attention to her plight, and says "I want public exposure for the unpardonable neglect of people who are possessed by a demon".
Issue 393: Jan 25th 2003

The New Age guru Deepak Chopra has thought of a way to liberate Iraq without further bloodshed. US troops should build a Disney World in Baghdad. "Let children breathe free at a place where fun and joy abide," he says.
Issue 402: March 29th 2003

A bad-tempered Italian hotelier held his guests hostage after they dared to lodge a complaint. Guests at the Villa Pinuccia, near Naples, decided to protest about the dirty sheets on their beds, grimy bathrooms and inedible food. But when they approached owner Anello Aiello, he went berserk, shouting: "Right. That's it. I've had enough. No one is leaving", and locked the guests in the reception area. They were eventually rescued by the police, who are considering a charge of kidnapping.
Issue 413: June 14th 2003

Officials in Michigan have published a "scratch and sniff" brochure for people thinking of moving to the country. The leaflet, which smells of manure, is designed to warn city-folk of the realities of rural life.
Issue 423: August 23rd 2003

A US media tycoon paid to have a beach built at a Berlin hotel so that he could relax while learning German. Haim Saban arranged to have 400kg of sand and two sacks of seashells transported from the Isle of Sylt and poured over the floor of a conference room at the Adlon hotel because he didn't want to feel as if he were back at school.
Issue 425: Sept 6th 2003

Madame Tussaud's is facing stiff competition, says Heat magazine. Louis Tussaud's House of Wax has become a cult tourist attraction because of its appallingly unrealistic models of celebrities such as Posh and Becks, Cliff Richard and Kylie Minogue. "It's quite hard to make a model when you can't get the person in the studio," says a spokesman for the Blackpool museum. "We have to make sculptures from photos. Some are not perfect, but they are not as bad as they used to be."
Issue 436: Nov 22nd 2003

German singletons need no longer feel lonely at Christmas, thanks to a new wallpaper range featuring life-sized pictures of fake friends. The wallpaper – which depicts people looking at home in the bedroom, living room, kitchen and bathroom – has become a best-seller in Germany. "The friends we provide are not very talkative, but they are guaranteed not to argue with you at Christmas," says designer Susanne Schmidt. Next, she hopes to bring out a range of personalised "partner wallpapers", for people who only see their loved-ones at weekends.
Issue 441: Dec 27th 2003

The world's first dwarf-dating reality TV show is about to be aired in America. Fox TV's The Littlest Groom will feature a dozen dwarf women competing with average-sized females for the affections of a 4ft 5in bachelor.
Issue 447: Feb 14th 2004

Santa Fe legislators are considering a law that would require pets to wear seat belts in the car. "Just like people need to be safe, so do animals," says Kate Rindy of the Santa Fe Animal Shelter, who helped write the bill. The law would require that cats, dogs and ferrets "be tethered or restrained so the animal can't fly out of the window".
Issue 455: April 10th 2004

A football fan travelled 4,700 miles from Everest to watch his favourite team lose. Mike Bromfield was 17,000 feet up Mount Everest when he heard, via his satellite phone, that Yeovil Town might make the play-offs. The 55-year-old tour guide immediately turned round, hiked for 72 hours through blizzards to reach an airstrip, flew to Kathmandu, caught a plane to Heathrow and rushed to Somerset just in time to watch Yeovil Town lose 2-1 against Hull City in the Third Division Match. "That's commitment," said a spokesman for the club.
Issue 461: May 22nd 2004

Serbian pensioners will soon be able to arm themselves with a walking stick which fires blank bullets and releases retractable blades at the touch of a button. The 007-style gadget, unveiled at an inventors' fair in Belgrade, also boasts a compass to help the elderly find their way home, a medicine dispenser and a panic button to call for help. Miladin Nikolic, 62, had the idea after he was attacked by stray dogs. "I didn't want any more nasty surprises," he says. "You should see the dogs run when I come down the road now."
Issue 462: May 29th 2004

A Bradford couple have decided to move offices after failing to stop a neighbour embarrassing their staff by pretending to have sex with a blow-up sheep and pig. Patricia and Graham Wadsworth decided to move their insurance broking business after a judge ruled their eccentric neighbour's daily performances from hi bedroom window were not in breech of the law.
Issue 466: June 26th 2004

Japanese designers have come up with the perfect bedtime accessory for single women – the Boyfriend Arm Pillow. The £43 pillow, which promises to hug its owner all night, comes in three colours of shirt, and has a built-in alarm clock feature, gently shaking the sleeper awake. The Boyfriend Arm Pillow is currently available only in Japan, but manufacturers Kameo are hoping to export it to the UK.
Issue 472: August 7th 2004

The entire population of an east Romanian village fled in panic after mistaking disco lights for an alien invasion. The villagers thought they were under attack by creatures from outer space when they saw neon lights in the sky. But police traced the lights to an outdoor disco in a nearby town, and persuaded them to return home. "We were so happy when we heard we had escaped an alien invasion," said one resident.
Issue 481: Oct 9th 2004

An Indian librarian has vowed to come to work semi-naked until his job is made permanent. For the last two weeks, Achal Singh has been working in Morena library, Madhya Pradesh, in only his underpants and one slipper. The 43-year-old is protesting about the fact that he is still a temporary employee after 12 years at the library. "I will not wear clothes until I get justice," he says.
Issue 482: Oct 16th 2004

An Oklahoma teacher hired two of his students to break into his house so he could impress his wife by fighting them off. Trent Spencer, 27, paid the teenagers $100 each to tie up his wife with duct tape and attempt to make off with the stereo. Spencer then came home and attacked the boys with a piece of wood that had been pre-cut so as to break in half on impact. But while the mock-fight was in progress, his wife managed to free herself and called the police. When officers arrived, the schoolboys confessed everything. Mr Spencer has been charged with filing a false report.
Issue 484: Oct 30th 2004

A robber who escaped from a prison in North Carolina has been found hiding out in a branch of Toys'R'Us. Jeffrey Manchester spent several months living in the store. He built himself a den under a staircase, put up spiderman posters, installed a portable nappy disposal unit as his lavatory, and even fitted a smoke alarm. He whiled away the time playing games off the shelves and lived off stolen baby food. "You hate to compliment the guy, because he's a dirt bag," said one police officer. "But we can learn a lot from him."
Issue 496: Jan 29th 2005

A Middlesborough man has been banned from service stations after becoming addicted to petrol. Brian Taylor, 36, sneaked on to one forecourt 51 times to drink from the pumps. He went to meetings to try to beat the habit– but stank so strongly of petrol that he was deemed a fire hazard and kicked out. Taylor was given an ASBO after being caught on CCTV downing four-star at an Asda garage, then dancing a jig while high. "He has become a real nuisance," said local policeman Sgt Bryan Tams.
Issue 498: Feb 12th 2005

Serbia's deputy culture minister has admitted sending secret agents to London to steal parts from the waxworks at Madame Tussaud's. Vladimir Tomcic said he wanted to ensure that the materials used in his country's wax museum were as good as at the London attraction. His spies stole two fingers from an unidentified waxwork.
Issue 502: March 12th 2005

A Texas artist has had his nose pierced with a metal bar to hold up his glasses. James Sooy, 22, got fed up with his glasses constantly sliding down his nose, so he had an inch-long metal bar inserted through the bridge. He uses magnets to attach a pair of rimless lenses to the bar. Sooy hopes to patent the invention and sell his frameless glasses for up to $100 a pair. "It's something people find interesting," he says, "but it's only for a certain few."
Issue 508: April 23rd 2005

A German travel agency is offering holidaymakers lessons in how to have fun. The courses, available in Hamburg, Munich and Dresden, include pointers on how to relax and forget about work. "They need to be reminded how to do simple things," says holiday trainer Irmgard Steiner, "like building sandcastles with their children or massaging sun cream on their partner."
Issue 513: May 28th 2005

When Annette Pharris's son Landon turned 16, she decided to get him a present he would never forget – a naked lady. Mrs Pharris and her husband, Landon Snr, hired "Sassy the stripper" to perform explicit dances for their son and 30 of his friends and family. Last week the couple from Nashville, Tennessee, were sentenced to two years' probation for contributing to the delinquency of a minor, and ordered to go to parenting classes. But Mrs Pharris remains defiant. "It's a bunch of bull," she says. "It didn't harm him. Even his grandpa was there. Anyway, let he who is without sin cast the first stone."
Issue 520: July 16th 2005

Farmers in Uttar Pradesh have lodged a complaint against their neighbour, who keeps eating their mud. Barsaatu Lal, from the village of Karimpur Bind, developed a taste for mud eight years ago. "I felt this sudden urge to eat mud," explains the 35-year-old. "I liked what I ate. Slowly, the quantity increased and today I eat nearly two kilograms of mud. I think it really benefits me and I feel immense strength when I eat it." Neighbouring farmers, however, complain that he keeps scoffing quality mud from their land. "We want to request the government to kindly grant him an acre of land so that he digs there only and eats to his gratification," says village elder Raj Bahadur.
Issue 530: Sept 24th 2005

A German company has outlawed moaning in its offices. Employees at IT firm Nutzwerk Ltd in Leipzig are contractually obliged to come to work in a good mood. "We made the ban on grumpiness official after one employee refused to subscribe to the company's philosophy of always smiling," said manager Thomas Kuwatsch. "She used to moan so much that other employees complained about her complaining. Once it was part of the contract, however, our employees really started to think more positively."
Issue 537: Nov 12th 2006

Officials in Malibu have distributed pamphlets warning surfers not to try to surf on a tidal wave if one hits California. "We want to encourage people to move away from the coast rather than toward it," explained Brad Davis, Malibu's director of emergency preparedness.
Issue 538: Nov 19th 2005

A Swiss driver who was flashed by a speed camera avenged himself by attacking it with a pickaxe, running over it with his car and then throwing it off a cliff. The motorist was driving through the village of La Punt Chamues-ch in the Alps when the camera flashed him. In a fury, he used a pickaxe to smash it free from its mountings. He then backed over it, put what was left of it in the car and drove up a mountain to hurl it off a cliff. Although the film and camera were destroyed, police spotted him as he threw it over the edge. He faces a £13,000 fine for destruction of public property.
Issue 540: Dec 3rd 2005

The Japanese town of Aioi is in mourning after someone decapitated "Gutsy Radish" – a vegetable that became a local hero when it was found growing valiantly through a stretch of asphalt. An unknown assailant cut the head off the radish, prompting tearful vigils and nationwide TV coverage. Gutsy Radish's severed head is now on hydroponic life-support in the town hall, where gardeners are hoping to stabilise it for replanting. "People discouraged by tough times were cheered by its strong will to live," said a town spokesman.
Issue 540: Dec 3rd 2005

An extreme marathon winner perplexed onlookers when she crossed the finishing line and carried on running, without stopping to claim the first prize. The unnamed woman vanished into the distance after winning the 24-hour race in Vienna. It was later revealed that she had pulled a sickie from work to compete in the race and was worried that colleagues would see her on television if she stopped.
Issue 545: Jan 14th 2006

Rich Americans are leaving money to themselves in the hope that they will one day be brought back to life. After arranging for their bodies to be cryogenically frozen, they put their wealth into "personal revival trusts", to be withdrawn when they are revived in a few centuries' time. David Pizer, 64, from Arizona, has left himself $10m and says that, after interest, he will wake up "the richest man in the world".
Issue 549: Feb 11th 2006

A retired cabinetmaker from Lancashire has spent six years and £30,000 turning his sitting room into a Baroque masterpiece. Dennis Nelems, who lives with his wife Norma in a two-bedroom retirement flat near Blackpool, has covered every inch with gilded cornices, pillars, sculptures and biblical frescoes. "I can't stand beige carpets and walls," he explained.
Issue 549: Feb 11th 2006

Towering Achievements

Han Qizhi was wearing jeans and ordinary footwear, had no safety equipment and had never climbed before, but as he walked past the 88-storey Jinmao Tower in Shanghai he thought he'd have a go. Hands raw and bloody, the shoe peddler was arrested after scaling the world's third tallest skyscraper in high winds and billowing fog. "If I fell, I'd not only have hurt myself but also my family and maybe pedestrians below," he said later from his cell. "I won't do this again."
Issue 303: April 21st 2001

An American company has come up with a novel toy designed to stimulate children's imaginations. "Invisible Jim" is simply an empty box costing £2.
Issue 309: June 2nd 2001

A Mexican widow has become the world's richest woman after putting £16,000 in the Banco del Atlantico in 1988. During the Mexican financial crisis of 1994, interest rates rose to 150% with the result that Celia Reyes is now worth £30bn. Despite a legal appeal, a court has ordered the bank to pay the full amount – more than Mexico's entire foreign currency reserves.
Issue 315: July 14th 2001

British businessman Troy Louis was enjoying a quiet spot of fishing on the River Ebro in Spain when he hooked an 11-stone catfish, reports The Sun. Louis, who was using bread and maggots for bait, took more than an hour to land the monster. "I'm still in shock," he told the paper.
Issue 328: Oct 13th 2001

A Romanian woman has created a collection of clothes using her own hair. Ioana Cioanca has just finished crocheting a raincoat to go with her brown blouse and skirt. "I already have a costume, a waistcoat, a hat, a shawl, a handbag and even a purse, all made from my own hair," she says. Ioana, 64, has been keeping her hair since she was 17 because her grandmother told her it was a sin to throw it away.
Issue 337: Dec 15th 2001

An illiterate butcher has won a place at Brazil's leading university after ticking answers at random in a multiple choice test. Severino Da Silva – who feigned sickness to get out of the essay paper – came ninth out of 1,000 applicants. His performance was described as "stunning" by examiners at Estacio de Sa University. He now hopes to study law.
Issue 338: Dec 22nd 2001

A dispute has broken out over who has the world's longest ear hair. The Guinness Book of Records announced earlier this year that the title belonged to B.D. Tyagi of Madhya Pradesh, India, whose ear hair is 10.2cm long. But now a farmer from the Indian state of Orissa claims to have cultivated two 13cm strands. Narayan Prasad Pal, 65, says: "I am proud of my hair. I want to have the record until I die. Other than this I have not achieved much in life."
Issue 350: March 23rd 2002

Peter Nowak, a pensioner from Pennsylvania, is almost certainly the stingiest man in the world. He admits that he cleans and reuses his dental floss, washing each strip in alcohol before hanging it up to dry. In this way he saves $3.50 a year. Nowak has now won the Philadelphia Inquirer's Cheapskate of the Year competition, beating into second place a man who goes to the funerals of strangers to get free food.
Issue 352: April 6th 2002

Britain's Tony Evans has spent five years creating the world's biggest rubber-band ball. Evans, 53, used six million rubber bands to assemble the ball, which stands 4ft 8in high and weighs 2,500lbs. Evans has beaten the world record, held by a group of 10,000 Americans, but his wife Liz wants the eyesore out of her garden. "I never want to see it again," she said.
Issue 361: June 8th 2002

Ten thousand Village People fans gathered in Livermore, Pennsylvania, to try to break the world record for the largest group rendition of 'YMCA'. The giant throng filled two football pitches in an effort to better Missouri's 1997 record of 6,907 singers. If the numbers are verified, it will be Livermore's second world record: the town is already home to the world's longest-burning light bulb.
Issue 366: July 13th 2002

The world's loudest burper has failed to break his own record. Paul Hunn, a solicitor's clerk from north London, was trying to top his record-setting 118.1 decibel burp. But with Guinness World Record officials on hand to record the proceedings, Hunn only managed 110.5 decibels, comparable in volume to a pneumatic drill or an aircraft taking off. Hunn says he will return to training and try again next year.
Issue 370: August 10th 2002

A Texas man has set the world record for the most number of grapes caught by mouth. Steve Spaulding, 40, caught 55 grapes in his mouth in one minute at a wine festival in Dallas. He then topped that feat by catching 1,189 grapes in 30 minutes; he also caught grapes thrown from a 22-storey hotel.
Issue 377: Sept 27th 2002

A group of Belgian women has broken the record for making the world's longest bra chain. The women, from the village of Westerlo, constructed a three-mile-long chain out of 7,400 bras, breaking the previous record – a 1.3-mile chain – set by the women of Bruges. The chain, which has been hung in the streets, has attracted 14,000 visitors so far.
Issue 378: Oct 5th 2002

A man in Rajasthan has been attracting huge crowds by chain-smoking through his ears. Dharmendra Singh can smoke up to 20 cigarettes in a row using his ears. "Initially I thought he was doing something wrong," says his father Amar. "But after reading about him in the newspapers I feel that he has done something good. He smokes through his ears. That's a big thing."
Issue 385: Nov 23rd 2002

An Indian man has broken the world record for having the most letters published in newspapers. Subhash Chandra Agrawal has had 1,226 letters published in India's national daily newspapers, beating the previous record of 602. The 53-year-old began writing letters to editors in 1967. "No issue is too trivial for me," said Subhash.
Issue 389: Dec 21st 2002

A town in Nevada is to host an "armpit festival" after being labelled the armpit of America by the Washington Post. The Festival of the Pit, in the town of Battle Mountain, will feature an armpit beauty pageant, a sweaty T-shirt competition and an antiperspirant contest. The town has already erected billboards along the main road reading: "Battle Mountain, Voted the Armpit of America by The Washington Post".
Issue 409: May 17th 2003

A Thai woman has won the Miss Drunk title in Bangkok. Arunothai Sriaran drank ten pints of wine and navigated a zig-zag obstacle course in seven seconds, wearing traditional Thai dress, to defeat 14 other hopefuls.
Issue 394: Feb 1st 2003

A British artist has been named the most boring photographer in the world after taking 1,000 pictures of cement mixers. Ronnie Crossland, 59, who has spent the last 15 years travelling 200,000 miles in search of the machines, says they are things of "great beauty". Crossland used to be a trainspotter, but gave it up because he found it too dull.
Issue 411: May 31st 2003

A Leicestershire man is selling his flat for $1.7m after spending the last ten years turning it into an exact replica of the Starship Enterprise. Tony Alleyne, who started the project as therapy after his wife left him, has built a life-size transporter control, a giant warp core drive and an infinity mirror. The flat also features voice-activated lighting and security. "If you have to do something," says Alleyne, "you should go all the way."
Issue 414: June 14th 2003

A 26-year-old Chinese woman has beaten 50 of her countrywomen to the title of Miss Ugly 2003. Zhang Di is looking forward to claiming her prize: £7,000 of plastic surgery. "My small eyes, flat nose and poor skin have been such a burden to me," she said.
Issue 439: Dec 13th 2003

A man has fulfilled his pledge to surf in California every day for 28 years. On Friday 29 February 1976, Dale Webster vowed to make a daily pilgrimage into the waves until the next time a Leap Day fell on the fifth Sunday in February. Webster, 55, surfed on his wedding day, took night jobs to keep his mornings free, and never went on holiday. He needs surgery to remove calcium deposits from his ears, and his eyes have some scar tissue from years of looking into the sun – but he holds the world record, having surfed for 10,407 days.
Issue 451: March 13th 2004

A man who scooped more than £6m on the German lottery didn't claim the money for ten weeks, because he wasn't sure he wanted it. The clerk from Dortmund, who wishes to remain anonymous, picked all six correct numbers in the draw on 3 January, entitling him to a £6,360,000 jackpot. When he failed to claim his winnings, WestLotto launched a poster campaign to find him. "I needed some time to think things through in peace," he said when he finally presented his ticket.

Issue 453: March 27th 2004

A ten-year-old boy is celebrating after winning a competition to find the smelliest feet in America. Daegan Goodman beat eight other finalists in the annual Rotten Sneaker Contest, judged by George Aldrich, a Nasa scent expert. "The stench has stayed with me for days," says Aldrich.

Issue 454: April 3rd 2004

An engineer from Kent has been crowned the world's fastest text-messager. James Trusler, 30, who emigrated to Australia six years ago, took a minute and seven seconds to send this message: "The razor-toothed piranhas of the genera Serrasalmus and Pygocentrus are the most ferocious freshwater fish in the world. In reality they seldom attack a human." Trusler, who sends more than 100 texts a day, performed the feat live on Australian TV, without having seen the text beforehand, to become the official Guinness World Records champion.

Issue 460: May 15th 2004

George Reiger's obsession is written all over him – literally. The 50-year-old postal worker is Disney's biggest fan. He has 1,643 tattoos of Disney characters on his body, including all 101 Dalmatians on his back. He also has 19,000 Disney collectables at his home in Santa Ana, California, and has been to Disney World 379 times – six of them on honeymoons. "My love for Disney comes first" he says. "That's why I've been through so many wives."

Issue 473: August 14th 2004

A petite 37-year-old saw off all comers at the World Lobster Eating Contest in Maine last week. Sonya Thomas, who weighs a mere seven-and-a-half stone, wolfed down 38 lobsters in just 12 minutes to win the award. Her competitors included Eric Booker, the 30-stone world doughnut, burrito and chocolate bar champion. "You'd think I could eat all of Sonya's food in a competition, and eat up Sonya, too," said Booker. "But size don't matter in this sport."

Issue 475: August 28th 2004

An Indian man is hoping to get into the record books by feeding a live cobra through his nose and out of his mouth. Charles Manoharan, aka 'Snake Manu', of Tamil Nadu, has been practising his routine with a garden snake. Manu, 25, says he has tried 'snake flossing' with kraits, sand boas and rat snakes, but his favourite is the cobra because of its "ferociousness and agility". He already holds a Guinness World Record for eating 200 worms in 30 seconds.

Issue 478: Sept 18th 2004

Gourmets from around the world have gathered in Serbia for the World Testicle Cooking Championships. The contest, in the village of Sabinac, is designed to promote the culinary delights of testicles, which are a local speciality. "The best cooked balls come from Serbia and we wanted to show the world what great dishes can be cooked using testicles," said Ljubomir Erovic of the Serbian Tourist Board.

Issue 486: Nov 13th 2004

A Chilean man has won a car by kissing it for 54 hours. Jose Aliaga, 22, was handed the keys after his last remaining rival in the 27-strong competition fainted. "My desire for the car was stronger," he explained.

Issue 493: Jan 8th 2005

A new high-adrenaline sport is taking off: extreme accounting. In an attempt to dispel their boring image, accountants everywhere are travelling all over the world, challenging one another by number-crunching on mountaintops, seabeds, caves and rollercoasters. "It's a phenomenon that pushes accountants to their limits – and beyond," says a spokesman for the Chartered Institute of Management Accounting.

Issue 504: March 26th 2005

A Slovenian TV programme that aimed to prove models were brainless bimbos had to be cancelled after one of its participants was found to be a genius. Iris Mulej was tested on her problem-solving abilities and spatial awareness. She scored 156 – higher than some of the scientists testing her, and well above the national average of 100. The producers are now hoping to do a different show, about the world's cleverest model.

Issue 506: April 9th 2005

A postman has won the 25th annual Ernest Hemingway lookalike contest on his 13th attempt. Bob Doughty, from Florida, beat 150 white-bearded rivals, all dressed like the author, at the contest in Key West. Doughty, 61, thanked "longevity". Hemingway's son Richard entered the competition last year, but failed to reach the final.

Issue 523: August 6th 2005

The very first shrine to ugly people is to be unveiled in a town known locally as the ugliness capital of the world. The statue of an unattractive man looking in the mirror will be unveiled in Piobbico in Italy as part of the festival of ugly people. "Everyone can come and look into the mirror and see for themselves if they are ugly too," said Telesforo Iacobellu, president of the world association for ugly people.

Issue 527: Sept 3rd 2005